THE NELSON AND HELEN GLUECK
COLLECTION OF CYPRIOT
ANTIQUITIES, CINCINNATI
BY
GISELA WALBERG

WITH A BIOGRAPHY
OF NELSON GLUECK
BY
REUBEN G. BULLARD

PAUL ÅSTRÖMS FÖRLAG

JONSERED 1992

739.382

WI5In

AAQ—4989

THE NELSON AND HELEN GLUECK
COLLECTION OF CYPRIOT
ANTIQUITIES, CINCINNATI
BY
GISELA WALBERG

WITH A BIOGRAPHY
OF NELSON GLUECK
BY
REUBEN G. BULLARD

PAUL ÅSTRÖMS FÖRLAG
JONSERED 1992

739.382

WI5In

AAQ—4989

Table of Contents

Table of Contents

Preface

I first saw the Nelson and Helen Glueck collection in connexion with a class on Cypriot archaeology which I taught in the early 1980's. Professor Cedric Boulter and his wife, Pat, as well as Dr. Carl I. Wyler had told me about its existence and Helen Glueck generously agreed to show it to me and my graduate students. I was impressed by the chronological range covered by the collection as well as by the quality of some of the objects. It was obvious to me that the collection should be made available to a wider public. Later I had the opportunity to get to know Helen Glueck as a scholar and friend through the Graduate Fellows of the University of Cincinnati. She invited me to her apartment to study the collection in detail and during my visits told me about her husband and his expeditions to the Near East. It was a great privilege to go through the collection together with her and to learn about its background. It became obvious to me that a publication of the collection should include a biography of Nelson Glueck. Dr. Reuben Bullard of the Cincinnati Bible College and the University of Cincinnati, who worked with Dr. Glueck as a graduate student, had often mentioned episodes from the time when they worked together in the field, and I therefore asked him to write the biography. His son, Reuben (Rick) Bullard Jr. made the excellent photographs of the objects in the collection. Mrs. M. Reichert and Mrs. S. Lucas of the Skirball Museum, Hebrew Union College went to much trouble, taking the objects from the Glueck Collection in their museum out of show cases and even out of storage when their collections were packed up before being shown in new premises. I wish to thank all those who helped me in the study and writing of this book.

The funds for this publication were provided by the Semple Fund of the Department of Classics, University of Cincinnati. I am indebted to Helen Glueck for the cost of the photography. The book is dedicated to her and to the memory of Nelson Glueck.

Cincinnati, October 8th 1991

Gisela Walberg

Abbreviations

AA	Archäologischer Anzeiger
Acts 1973	Acts of the International Archaeological Symposium, The Mycenaeans in the Eastern Mediterranean, Nicosia 1973
Acts 1986	Acts of the International Archaeological Symposium, Cyprus Between the Orient and the Occident, Nicosia 1986
BICS	Bulletin of the Institute of Classical Studies
BSA	British School at Athens, Annual
CAH	Cambridge Ancient History
OpusAth	Opuscula Atheniensia
RDAC	Report of the Department of Antiquities, Cyprus
SCE	The Swedish Cyprus Expedition
SIMA	Studies in Mediterranean Archaeology

Introduction

This small but interesting collection of Cypriot vases was made by Dr. Nelson Glueck and his wife Helen during their frequent visits to the Near East during the 1930s to 1950s.

The twenty-eight vases and five figurines in the collection range from the Early Bronze Age to the Cypro-Archaic period (c. 1900-475 B.C.). Five vases and one figurine (nos. 28-33) are at present at the Skirball Museum of the Hebrew Union College, Cincinnati, where Dr. Glueck was the president for many years.

Many of the vases do not have an exact provenance but where evidently found on Cyprus and in the Levant. The provenance given in the catalogue is taken from notes kept by Dr. Glueck. Where the provenance is known, it is noted in the catalogue. The collection reflects the early interrelations between Cyprus and the Near East during almost two thousand years. The end of the Early Bronze Age and the beginning of the Middle Bronze Age on Cyprus (Early Cypriot III - Middle Cypriot I) - a time to which some of the earliest vases in the collection (nos. 1-3) are datable - was a time of significant changes on Cyprus. The culture became less provincial than before. There are more and larger settlements than before, especially in the northern and central parts of the Island, and the process of urbanization seems to have begun. The economy, which was based on agriculture, metallurgy and hunting, was flourishing. Copper mining and industry was beginning to develop during this period. Finds of imported Cretan vases in Cypriot tombs may reflect the establishment of trade connexions with the Aegean. Faience beads were imported from Egypt. The predominant ceramic wares of this period were red or black with a polished surface often with incised panels (see nos. 1-3).

During the second part of the Middle Bronze Age (Middle Cypriot II), Cypriot pottery was exported to the Levant and other parts of the Near East. Pottery was also imported to the island from abroad. Copper was exported. A place called Alasia which may be Cyprus is mentioned on 17th century tablets from Mari in Syria as a copper-producing area. The most frequent ware of this period is white and decorated with dark paint, so-called White Painted Ware (see no. 4). The ceramic decoration of this period is often very elaborate.

The construction of a number of fortresses, destructions of settlements, mass burials and plundered tombs indicate that the end of the Middle Bronze Age on Cyprus was violent. The reason for the destructions, which coincide with the Hyksos period in Egypt are unknown. They may, possibly, be connected with an invasion of the island. The political conditions seem to have been similar at the beginning of the Late Bronze Age, c. 1650-1550 B.C. It has been suggested that the reason for unrest may have been antagonism between eastern and western Cyprus over the control of the copper mines in the Troodos mountains and of the arable land in the East. Mass-burials in the northern part of the island are, however, usually explained by an epidemic. From c. 1550 B.C. the situation seems to have improved. The 18th Dynasty was established in Egypt and more peaceful conditions seem to have returned in the East Mediterranean. A number of harbour towns were built along the coast (Enkomi, Hala Sultan Tekke, Maroni, Morphou and Ayia Irini) from which Cypriot pottery and copper were exported. It is unclear whether the copper industry was organized by different coastal towns or whether there was some central authority and organization. Rural sites also developed in the centre of the island. Copper slag has been found at almost every site from this period. The copper was exported in the shape of ingots. Tin must have been imported from elsewhere. At this time Cyprus had close commercial contacts with the Aegean and the Near East. With the establishment of more peaceful conditions, two new ceramic wares appear on the island: White Slip ware (see no. 15) which has a smooth surface covered with a thick white slip decorated with orange and brown paint and Base Ring ware (see nos. 5-11, 29-30) which has thin walls, a dark shiny surface with relief decoration and a metallic character. Late Base-Ring ware is decorated with white paint. Both wares are handmade. They were exported to the Near East in large quantities and were evidently very popular there. The potter's wheel had been in use for a long time in these areas and, consequently, the handmade Cypriot pottery may have had an exotic appeal. Mycenaean pottery was imported from the Greek Mainland to Cyprus and also to the Near East (see nos. 13-14). Near Eastern Red Lustrous Wheelmade was probably imported to Cyprus at the beginning of the Late Bronze Age, but was later made on Cyprus and exported from there to the Near East.

At the end of the second phase of the Late Bronze Age (Late Cypriot II), c. 1225 B.C., many settlements on Cyprus were destroyed. These destructions coincide with destructions at a number of sites on the Greek Mainland. The island seems to have been colonized by Mycenaeans who introduced monumental architecture and Mycenaean pottery, which soon was imitated on the island. Late Mycenaean (LH IIIC) pottery has also been found in the Near East. Local Cypriot wares now included bucchero (see no. 17) and wheelmade wares. Later, after 1175 B.C., Proto

White Painted ware (see no. 16) appeared on the Island. Scholars have connected it with another wave of immigrants from the Greek Mainland who seem to have brought an Arcadian dialect of Greek with them. Now Cypriot pottery was not exported to any large extent to the Near East or elsewhere.

At the end of the Bronze Age, c. 1050 B.C., many settlements on Cyprus were destroyed and abandoned. New cities, such as Salamis and Palaeopaphos, were built at the beginning of the Iron Age. The construction of these new cities is often ascribed in foundation legends to Greek heroes who came to Cyprus "after the Trojan War". Iron was used for knives, daggers and, finally, also swords, even though copper was still traded. The period coincides with the transition from the Sub-Mycenaean to the Proto-Geometric period in the Aegean. A homogeneous Cypro-Geometric culture developed. It has been divided into three different phases: Cypro-Geometric I (c. 1050-950 B.C), Cypro-Geometric II (c. 950-850 B.C.) and Cypro-Geometric III (c. 850-700 B.C.). Cyprus had close contacts with the Near East which gradually increased during this period. Syro-Palestinian pottery (Black-on-Red ware) which is covered with red slip and decorated with black paint was first imported during Cypro-Geometric I. Later, this ware was produced on Cyprus and eventually exported to the Near East (see nos. 26, 34). White Painted ware (see nos. 20, 22, 25), decorated with matt black paint on a light surface developed from Proto-White Painted ware and continued to be popular. Bichrome ware (see nos. 18 19, 21, 23, 33) which is closely related to White Painted ware, was also produced. It is decorated with red and black paint. Black Slip ware (see no. 32) was used mainly for jugs. Many simply made, painted terracotta figurines were produced during the Cypro-Geometric as well as during the

Cypro-Archaic period (see nos. 26-28, 35). The Phoenician influence on Cyprus was strong during the Cypro-Geometric period, and the city of Kition was colonized by Phoenicians from Tyre. The rest of the island consisted of many small kingdoms.

The Cypro-Geometric period probably ended and the Cypro-Archaic period started some time before 707 B.C., when the island was reduced to submission by the Assyrians. Cypro-Archaic I, c. 700-600 B.C., represents one of the most flourishing periods in ancient Cyprus. As before, the island was divided into several independent kingdoms. Overseas trade was more extensive than ever. Cypriot trading posts were founded in Syria, Cilicia, Egypt and Rhodes, and Cypriot pottery was exported to all these areas. At the same time, Egyptian objects especially were imported to Cyprus. It is possible that Cypriot and Phoenician merchants worked together. There is a particularly strong Phoenician influence on Cyprus from c. 650 B.C. when Tyre was attacked by the Assyrians and Phoenician refugees seem to have settled on the island.

The Glueck collection of Cypriot vases is an excellent study collection which reflects the history of Cyprus and the relations between Cyprus and the Near East. Helen Glueck has often generously made it available to Bronze Age students from the Department of Classics at the University of Cincinnati, to students from Hebrew Union College and to visiting scholars. This pocket-book in the SIMA-series is meant to make it available to a wider public.

Catalogue

Bronze Age

1. 29. Red Polished III Juglet

H. 10.2 cm.; d. of rim 3.8 cm.; d. of body 9.5 cm.

Some chips are missing from the rim.

Low maximum diameter. Handle from rim to shoulder.

On the body is a network, formed by concentric circle motifs and between them groups of connecting diagonal and horizontal lines. The lowest circle motifs are connected by a horizontal band, consisting of groups of seven lines. Opposite the handle, on both sides, above the horizontal band, are two plant-like motifs, formed by rows of oblique lines. Underneath the handle is a vertical row of seven incised lines. Much white filling still remains in the incised lines.

Clay: 2.5YR 6/4; slip 10R 5/6.

Type I B 3 d 1 var. a.

Cf. SCE IA, Fig. XCIII:5.

Provenance: unknown.

Date: EC III-MC I.

2. 57. Black Polished Bowl

H. 6.5 cm.; d. 10.2 cm.

Semiglobular body; pierced stringhole at the rim.

The vase is decorated on the exterior, beneath the rim with a horizontal band of repeated lozenges, filled with short, transverse strokes and framed above and below by horizontal lines. The rest of the vase is divided into four fields by crossing. cross-hatched bands. At the centre of the base, there is a reserved square. In each field is a group of three oblique rows of lozenges. There are traces of white paint in the incisions.

Clay: ?; slip 2.5YR N2.5.

Cf. SCE IV IA, Figs. CXL, CXLI; Frankel, nos. 10, 16-17.

Provenance: unknown.

Date: EC III-MC I.

3. 30. Black Polished Miniature Gourd Flask

H. 5.8 cm.; d. 3.8 cm.

Intact, but one side has a very worn surface.

Globular body. Tall, narrow neck, pierced by two small holes at the top.

On the neck. there are groups of incised, oblique lines. Below the neck is a horizontal band, consisting of five parallel lines. The main decoration is formed by a broad, horizontal zone of repeated lozenges, filled with oblique lines. Below this zone is a horizontal band, consisting of four lines. There are traces of white colour in the incised lines.

Clay: ?; slip 2.5YR N2.5.

Cf. SCE IV IA, Fig. CLII:20.

Provenance: unknown.

Date: EC III-MC I.

4. 166. White Painted IV Deep bowl

H. 9.3 cm.; d. of rim 6.2 cm.; d. of body 8 cm.

Intact. Irregular rim.

Depressed, semiglobular body; high, vertical handle from rim to body.

On the interior and exterior rim are double zigzag lines. The handle is decorated with double transverse lines in alternating directions and the sides of the handle are painted with parallel lines. At the base on the rim is a horizontal line. Beneath this line id a wide zone of triangles in alternating directions, filled with oblique lines, also drawn in alternating directions within each triangle. On the lower part of the vase is a wavy band. The base is decorated with a circle, divided into four parts by triple, crossing lines.

Clay: 5YR 7/3; slip 5YR 7/6 to 10YR 8/4; paint 10R 4/4.

Type III e.

Provenance: unknown.

Date: MC II.

5. 79. Base-ring I Jug

H. 26 cm.; d. of rim 8.3 cm.; d. of base 7.0 cm.; d. of body 13.5 cm.

Two fragments missing from the base.

Depressed, globular body; tall neck, widening towards the rim; flat handle from upper part of the neck to the shoulder; rim moulding; trumpet base. At the upper handle base are two horizontal ridges and at the base of the neck another, similar ridge. The handle is decorated with two incised, vertical lines. The decoration on the body consists of a pair of ridges in the form of antithetic J-spirals, opposite the handle.

Clay: 2.4YR 6/6; slip 2.5YR N4/.

Type: VI D 1 d Γ.

Cf. SCE IV 1C, Fig. XLIX:9.

Provenance: unknown.

Date: LC IB.

6. 76. Miniature Base-ring I Tankard

H. 10.3 cm.; d. of rim 5.5 cm.; d. of base 3.3 cm.; d. of body 7.3 cm.

Depressed, biconical body; wide neck; flat rim; flaring base; handle from rim to shoulder with a high thumb-grip. Around the neck are two horizontal ridges.

Clay: 10R 6/3; slip 2.5YR 6/6.

Type: similar to VII Β 1 .

Cf. SCE IV 1C, Fig. L:7.

Provenance: unknown.

Date: LC IC.

7. 78. Base-ring II Bowl

H. incl. handle 9.8 cm.; d. of rim 13 cm.; d. of base 5.3 cm.; d. of body 13.2 cm.

Intact.

Straight rim; slightly concave neck; angular shoulder; fork handle, ring-base.

Clay:?; slip 2.5YR 3/2 to 2.5YR 6/6.

Type: I F b.

Cf. SCE IV 1C, Fig. LII:4.

Provenance: unknown.

Date: LC II.

8. 81. Base-ring II Lentoid Flask

H. 18 cm.; d. 15 cm.; w. 7.8 cm.

Intact, but the surface is worn.

Rather convex body with a sharp, ridge-like flange along the edge of the body; narrow, tapering neck; plain rim; handle from the upper part of the neck to the shoulder. Traces of oblique, white lines in groups of four on the body.

Clay: 10R 6/4; slip 10R 4/1; paint 10YR 8/1.

Type: XIII a.

Cf. SCE IC 1C, Fig. LIII:13.

Date: LC II.

9. 80. Base-ring II Jug

H. 25.3 cm.; d. of rim 9.7 cm.;d. 9.2 cm.; d. of body 13.5 cm.

Intact.

Globular body; round mouth; tall neck; flaring rim and base; strap handle from the upper part of the neck to the shoulder; moulding at the base of the neck.

The handle is decorated with two parallel, incised, horizontal bands. On the neck are groups of horizontal lines in white. Below the neck-moulding is a group of five horizontal lines and the main decoration consists of a zigzag band, formed by five parallel lines. On the lower part of the body are two horizontal bands, consisting of five parallel lines. The upper of these bands is crossed by the lower part of the zigzag band.

Clay: ?; slip 2.5YR N4/; paint 10R 8/2.

Type: IX B d.

For the shape, cf. SCE IV 1C, Fig. LIII:1.

Provenance: unknown.

Date: LC II.

10. 74. Base-ring II Juglet

H. 15.5 cm.; d. of rim 3.0 cm.; d. of body 7.5 cm.

The rim is chipped.

Globular body; tall neck; strap handle from slightly below the rim to the shoulder; trumpet base. Decorated on the neck with horizontal, white lines and with oblique lines on the body.

Clay: ?; slip 2.5YR N4/; paint 10YR 8/2.

Type: IX B 1 b.

Cf. SCE IV 1C, Fig. LII:14b.

Provenance: Es Samia near Ramallah.

Date: LC II.

11. 83. Base-Ring II Animal-Shaped Vase

H. 15.8 cm.; l. 16.5 cm.

A portion of one leg is broken off as is the tip of one horn.

Handle from the back of the neck, where there is an opening at the upper handle-base, to the middle part of the back. Pointed, pierced nose. The eyes are represented by small pellets, surrounded by small, circular ridges. Below the horns are small ears. The tail is represented by a low ridge. The decoration consists of groups of horizontal, vertical and oblique white lines.

Clay: 5YR 6/4; slip 5YR 4/2; paint 10YR 8/3.

Type: XVI b.

Cf. SCE IV 1C, Fig. LIII:15.

Provenance: unknown.

Date: LC II.

12. Small White Shaved Jug

H. 10.5 cm., d. 4.7 cm.

Intact.

Pinched rim; spindle-shaped body with traces of trimming.

Provenance: unknown.

Date: LCIB-LCIIB.

13. 88. Mycenaean LH IIIA2 Lentoid Flask

H. 16.5 cm.; d. 13.4 cm.

Rim fragmentary.

Flat, lentoid body; short neck; flaring rim; opposite, horizontal handles.

The rim and handles are painted. Both sides of the body are decorated with concentric circle motifs, surrounding a central dot. The widest circle reaches up on the lower part of the neck.

Clay: 2.5YR 6/4; slip 5YR 8/2; paint 10R 4/3 to 4/4.

FS 186.

Cf. SCE IV 1C, Fig. LXXVII:11.

Provenance: unknown.

Date: 1400-1300 B.C.

14. 89. Mycenaean LH III A1 Piriform Jar

H. 18.7 cm.; d. of rim 10.2 cm.; d. of base 5.6 cm.; d. of body 14 cm.

Several fragments are missing from the rim and the base and two handles are broken off. The paint is much faded and worn off.

Piriform body; low, concave neck; thin, horizontal lip; three vertical handles; torus base.

The rim is decorated with horizontal bands. On the shoulder is a scale-pattern, FM 70:1, separated from the rest of the body by two horizontal bands. Further down on the body are two horizontal bands and above the base two more. The lowest part of the body, above the base is painted and as is the edge of the base.

Clay: 2.5YR 6/6; slip 10YR 8/3; paint 2.5YR 5/4.

FS 31.

Provenance: unknown.

Date: 1425-1400 B.C.

15. 90. White Slip II Bowl

H. 8.5 cm.; d. of rim 13.5 cm.; d. of body 13.5 cm.

One chip is missing from the rim. The handle is reset.

Semiglobular shape; wishbone handle.

The rim is decorated with a horizontal, cross-hatched band. From this band depend alternating broad and narrow vertical cross-hatched bands. Some of the colour on the exterior has stained the interior rim. Opposite the handle, on both sides of a broad, vertical band on the exterior are two vertical rows of dots. The upper part of the handle is decorated with transverse bands and lines. The underside has a line on each side, which cross at the tip of the handle.

Clay: ?; slip 10YR 8/4; paint 10R 3/3.

Type: I A.

Cf. SCE IV 1C, Fig. LXXXIII:8.

Provenance: unknown.

Date: LC II.

16. 93. Proto White Painted Stirrup Jar

H. 14.6 cm.; d. of base 4.6 cm.; d. of body 13.6 cm.

Intact.

Depressed globular, almost biconical body; the spout has a flaring rim; low foot. Small, pointed knob on the top disc.

The interior spout is painted. The top disc is decorated with an irregular circle. The handles are painted along the sides with vertical lines, connected by transverse strokes. The main decoration, on the shoulder, consists of irregular semicircles, FM 43:o. One of these semicircle motifs is framed by small dots or strokes. There are also small dots around the base of the right handle. The spout has four transverse strokes and its base is encircled by an irregular line. Beneath the semicircles is a horizontal band and on the lower part of the body are two more horizontal bands. The edge of the base is painted. The surface and paint are shinier than is usually the case in Proto White Painted pottery.

Clay: ?; slip 10YR 2/1 to 2.5YR 5/6.

FS 175.

Provenance: Ain Samia near Dura.

Date: LC IIIB-C.

17. 82. Bucchero Jug

H. 13.2 cm.; d. of rim 4.8 cm.; d. of base 5.0 cm.; d. of body   cm.

Chips are missing from the rim and the base. The body is scratched on one side.

Ovoid body; handle from rim to shoulder; short neck, which widens upwards; slightly flaring base.

Around the neck is a moulding and c. 1 cm. further down, the body is decorated with vertical grooves. The handle has a high central ridge.

Clay: 2.5YR 6/6; slip 2.5YR 5/2.

Type I B c.

Cf. SCE IV 1C, Fig. LXXVIII:2.

Provenance: unknown.

Date: LC III.

Iron Age

18. 103. Bichrome II Flask (Syrian?)

H. 13.8 cm.; d. 8.8 cm.; w. 6.3 cm.

Intact, but the surface is worn and the paint is almost completely faded away on one side while it is still visible on the other side.

Lentoid body; flaring rim; opposite vertical handles from the upper part of the neck to the shoulder.

On both sides of the body are concentric circle motifs, consisting of alternating red and black circles. The handles have short, black, transverse strokes.

Clay: 2.5YR 6/4; slip 5YR 7/3; black paint 5YR 4/1; red paint 10R 5/8.

Cf. SCE IV 2, Fig. XVI:11.

Provenance: unknown.

Date: Cypro-Geometric II.

19. 157. Bichrome II Plate

H. 2.2 cm; d. 12.2 cm.

Some chips are missing from the rim.

Opposite, horizontal handles.

The rim and the handles are painted black. On the exterior is a reserved band, filled with concentric circles in black. Further in, there is a broad red band and, again, a reserved band with concentric circles in black. The centre is marked by a black circle, 2.3 cm in diameter. On the interior, there are two circles in black, outlining the central part of the dish. At the centre is a small, black, unfilled circle.

Clay: 5YR 7/6; slip 10YR 8/4; black paint 10R 2.5; red paint 10R 4/6.

Cf. SCE IV 2, Fig.XV:8.

Provenance: unknown.

Date: Cypro-Geometric II.

20. 155. White Painted III Amphora

H. 34.5 cm.; d. of rim 12.5 cm.; d. of base 8 cm.; d. of body   cm.

Chips are missing from the rim, neck and the surface of the body.

Globular-conical body; opposite, horizontal handles on the shoulder, rounded rim.

The interior of the rim is decorated with two horizontal bands. The exterior is covered with paint, except for a reserved band of fourteen horizontal lines. This zone is framed above and below by broad horizontal bands. Below the base of the neck is another horizontal band and above the shoulder a group of seven horizontal lines. The handles are connected with a wavy line in a reserved zone. Beneath the shoulder zone is a group of seven horizontal lines and on the lower part of the body a broad, horizontal band.

Clay: 7.5YR 7/2; slip 10YR 7/4; paint 7.5YR N4/.

Cf. SCE IV 2, Fig XXIV:1 (Bichrome).

Provenance: El Husin.

Date: Cypro-Geometric III.

21. 150. Bichrome III Bowl

H. 8.6 cm.; d. 12.5 cm.

Chips are missing from the rim and one patch (c. 1.0 cm. of diameter) of slip near the rim has been scraped off.

Angular shape; flaring foot; ridge beneath the rim; small, horizontal handles. The upper part of the base shows parallel wheel-marks. The top of the rim is painted black. Further down, on the exterior, is a broad, red band and a black line. The handles are painted black and the paint continues beneath the handles. The main decoration on both sides consists of a bird motif with the body of the bird formed by a fish. It resembles a number of bird motifs published by Karageorghis and des Gagniers in La ceramique chypriote (cf., for instance, XXV.a.3-5), but in none of these bird motifs does the body of the bird consist of a fish. The decoration on this bowl in the Glueck Collection is unique and a product of the lively imagination of the vase-painter. The motif is outlined in black and filled with red paint. On each side of the bird motifs are groups of four vertical lines. At the height of the handle bases is a broad, black band, separating the upper and lower part of the vessel. The foot is encircled by a broad, black band. On the interior of the rim is a broad, red band. Beneath the band are three black horizontal lines. The centre of the interior is reserved and decorated with three concentric circles in black. It is surrounded by an area with red paint and black circles.

Clay: 7.5YR 7/6; slip 10YR 8/4; black paint 10R 3/1; red paint 10R 3/6.

Cf. SCE IV 2, Fig. XXI:7a-b.

Provenance: unknown.

Date: Cypro-Geometric III.

22. White Painted III Juglet

H. 10.8 cm; d. 6 cm.

Chip missing from the rim, otherwise intact.

Globular body, flat base.

On the neck are three horizontal lines and on the body three groups of concentric circles framing small dots.

Date: Cypro-Geometric III.

23. 167. Bichrome III Barrel-Shaped Jug.

H. 10.6 cm.; d. of body 7.3 cm.; w. of body 7.0 cm.

One chip is missing from the rim.

Slightly flattened body with small knobs in the centre of both sides; short neck.

Beneath the rim are four horizontal black lines and at the base of the neck, a broader band in black. The handle has vertical black bands on both sides, connected with short, black, transverse strokes. On both sides of the body are concentric circle motifs in alternating black and red (thin black lines and broader red bands). The knobs are painted black.

Clay: 5YR 7/6; slip 5YR 8/3; black paint 2.5YR 2.5/; red paint 10R 4/4.

Cf. SCE IV 2, Fig. XXII:6.

Provenance: unknown.

Date: Cypro-Geometric III.

24. 26. Black-On-Red II (IV) Bottle

H. 12 cm.; d. of rim 3.8 cm.; d. of body 7.3 cm.

Intact, but the paint on the rim is worn off.

Globular body.

The edge of the rim is painted. Beneath the rim the neck is encircled by a horizontal band and there is a second horizontal band at the handle ridge. The base of the neck is encircled by a third horizontal band. The handles are painted. On the shoulder, on each side, are two parallel concentric circle motifs. The body is encircled at the maximum diameter by a horizontal band, consisting of seven lines. Further down on the body are two broader horizontal bands.

Clay: 5YR 7/3; slip 2.5YR 5/8; paint 2.5YR N. 2.5/.

Cf. SCE IV 2, Fig. XXXIX:2.

Provenance: unknown.

Date: Cypro-Archaic I.

25. 165. White Painted IV jug

H. 12.3 cm.; d. of mouth from handle 4.6 cm.; d. of body 10 cm.

A small chip is missing from the mouth. There is also a crack at the lower handle base.

Low maximum diameter; pinched mouth; arched handle from rim to shoulder; ring base.

The rim is painted. On each side of the mouth are "eyes", consisting of a dot, surrounded by a circle. On the handle is a group of horizontal lines, an x-motif and, further down, a zigzag line. At the lower handle base is a large quirk. The neck is encircled by a horizontal band.

Opposite the handle is a group of three swastikas and beneath them another swastika. The edge

of the base is painted.

Clay: 10YR 8/3; slip 2.5YR 8/2; paint 2.5YR N3/.

Provenance: unknown.

Date: Cypro-Archaic I.

26. 159. Animal Figurine

H. 5.3 cm.; l. 10.3 cm.

Handmade in "snowman" technique.

Large, triangular head and tail; small, pointed ears; broad, flat legs; short tail.

Decorated with alternating black and red vertical bands.

Clay: ?; slip 5YR 8/3; black paint 5YR 3/1; red paint 10R 4/6.

Cf. Monloup, Salamine XII,2:5.

Provenance: unknown.

Date: Cypro-Geometric - Cypro-Archaic.

27. 91. Horseman Figurine

H. 10 cm.; l. 12.8 cm.

Handmade in "snowman" technique.

One leg is broken off and reset.

The man has a pointed headdress (helmet) and holds on to the neck of the horse with very broad, flat hands. His legs are smoothed down onto the horse's back. The horse has a long, large head, small, rounded ears and a short broad tail, turned to the left.

A red, v-shaped ornament is painted on the horseman's back. The helmet is painted red. The nose, eyes and chin have black transverse strokes. The legs of the horseman show traces of black paint. The horse has red ears, a red fringe on top of his head and one central red band, framed on each side by black bands from forehead to nose. The chest has red horizontal bands alternating with groups of double horizontal black lines and the hindquarters and the hindlegs are decorated with alternating red and black vertical lines.

Clay: 2.5YR 5/6; slip 7.5YR 7/2; black paint 10R 2.5; red paint 10R 4/4.

Cf. Monloup, Salamine XII, Pl. 10, nrs. 150-51.

Provenance: unknown.

Date: Cypro-Geometric - Cypro-Archaic.

28. Horseman Figurine

H. 16 cm. ;l.15 cm.

Intact.

Handmade in "snowman"technique.

The man has a pointed headdress (helmet) and holds on to the neck of the horse with broad, flat hands. No legs are represented. The horse has a high mane which stands up above the forehead and forms a high ridge along the neck.

The horseman's helmet is painted with a vertical red line which continues across his nose. There are traces of paint on his hands. The mane of the horse is painted black as well as the nose, ears and tail. Beneath the mane are traces of red paint.

Clay: ?; slip 7.5YR 8/2; paint 10R 4/3.

Cf. Monloup, Salamine XII, Pl. 10, nrs. 150-51.

Provenance: unknown.

Date: Cypro-Geometric - Cypro-Archaic.

In the Skirball Museum, Cincinnati Branch, Hebrew Union College

Bronze Age

29. Base-Ring II Flask

H. 14.3 cm.; w. 8.8 cm.; d. 5 cm.

Intact. Paint faded.

Lentoid body; slightly tilted neck; flat rim; handle from neck to shoulder.

Decorated with vertical and oblique white lines.

Clay: 2.5YR 6/2; slip 5YR 4/1; paint 5YR 7/2.

Type XIIIa.

Cf. SCE 1C, Fig. LIII:13, Biers, J. (SIMA XX:2) No. 37.

Provenance: unknown.

Date: LCII.

30. Base-Ring II Jug

H. 22 cm.; d. of rim 7.5 cm.; d. of body 13 cm.

One chip is missing from the rim and two from the base. Slip and paint is entirely worn off on one side.

Depressed globular body; strap handle from the upper part of the neck to the shoulder; cylindrical neck; flaring rim; neck-moulding; trumpet-base.

Decorated with groups of horizontal lines on the neck and with groups of vertical lines on the body.

Clay: 5YR 6/3; slip 2.5 YR 5/4 to 5YR 4/1; paint 5YR 7/2.

Cf. SCE IV IC, Fig. LIII:2.

Provenance: unknown.

Date: LC IB-IIB.

31. White Shaved Jug

H. 18.2 cm.; h. without handle 16.8 cm.

Spindle-shaped body; short, narrow neck; pinched mouth; slightly raised handle from rim to shoulder.

Clay: 2.5 YR 6/4.

Type I a.

Provenance: unknown.

Date: LC IB-IIB.

Iron Age

32. Black Slip II Juglet

H. 9.0 cm.; d. of mouth from the neck 3.7 cm.; d. of body 6.5 cm.

Chip missing from the base.

Globular body. Trefoil mouth.

Decorated with a group of five horizontal, incised lines on the shoulder and vertical grooves on the body.

Clay: 5YR 6/3; slip 5YR 4/1 to 5YR 5/2.

Cf. SCE IV 2, Fig. XVII:1.

33. Bichrome IV Juglet

H. 10 cm.; d. of rim 3.5 cm.; d. of body 6.6 cm.

Intact, but the paint on the rim is partly worn off and some of the red paint on the body is faded.

Globular body.

Only the lower part of the body is slipped.

Decorated on the rim with a red band. On the upper part of the neck is a broad, horizontal, red band, framed above and below by black lines. At the handle ridge is a horizontal black line and on the lower part of the body are two more black bands. The handle is painted in black on its upper side. On the lower side are some irregular, black, short, horizontal lines.

Opposite the handle is a vertical zone containing a triangle and a lozenge in black filled with short, transverse strokes. The lines which form the triangle and the lozenge, have been continued outwards and downwards to accentuate the decoration on the sides of the vase. This decoration consists of large, concentric circles in black and red.

Clay: 7.5 YR 7/2; slip 10YR 7/3; black paint 10YR 3/1; red paint 2.5YR 5/6 to 10YR 3/1.

Cf. SCE IV 2, Fig. XXXIII:9.

Date: Cypro-Archaic I.

34. Black-on-Red I (III) Juglet

H. 8.7 cm.; d. of rim 2.7 cm.; d. of body 5.3 cm.

Intact, but with irregular, mottled surface, largely black.

Globular body.

Decorated with a horizontal band around the neck and with a group of five horizontal lines at the height of the maximum diameter. Opposite the handle is a concentric circle motif.

Clay: ?; slip 10R 2.5/2.

Cf. SCE IV 2, Fig. XXV:10.

Provenance: unknown.

35. Small Dog-like Figurine

L. 11.0 cm.; h. 6.1 cm.

Handmade, "snow-man" technique.

The animal is holding its head up, as if begging. Triangular, fox-like tail.

Decorated with alternating red and black transverse strokes.

Clay: 7.5 YR 7/2; slip 10YR 7/2; black paint 10YR 4/1; red paint 4/6.

Cf. Monloup, Salamine XII, Pl. 2:15.

Provenance: unknown.

Date: Cypro-Geometric - Cypro-Archaic.

Bibliography

Adelman, C., Cypro-Geometric Pottery: Refinements in Classification, (SIMA XLVI) Gothenburg 1976

Artzy, M. F., "Imported and Local Bichrome Ware in Megiddo", Levant 10, 1978, 99 ff.

Åström, P., Excavations at Kalopsidha and Ayios Iakovos in Cyprus (SIMA II), Lund 1966

----------, "The Economy of Cyprus and its Development in the IInd Millenium" Archaeologia Viva II:3, 1969, 72 ff.

----------, The Middle Cypriot Bronze Age. The Late Cypriot Bronze Age. SCE IV (IB-ID, Lund 1972

----------, "The Sea Peoples in the Light of New Excavations", Centre d'Etudes Chypriotes 3, 8 ff.

----------, "Hala Sultan Tekke", Archaeology in Cyprus 1969-1985, 173 ff.

---------- & al., Hala Sultan Tekke 1-8 (SIMA XLV:1-8) Gothenburg 1976-83

Barlow, J.A., The Stratified Pottery of the Bronze Age Settlement at Alambra, Cyprus: a preliminary Report (Diss.) Ann Arbor 1985.

Begg, P., Late Cypriot Terracotta Figurines: a Study of Context, (SIMA Pocket-book 101), Gothenburg 1991

Biers, J.C., & al., The Cypriote Collection of the Museum of Art and Archaeology, University of Missouri-Columbia (SIMA XX:2), Gothenburg 1979

Bliquez, L. J., Cypriote Objects in Washington State (SIMA XX:6), Gothenburg 1975

Boardman, J., The Greeks Overseas, London 1980

Brunnsåker, S., & Säve-Söderbergh (eds.) From the Gustavianum Collections in Uppsala 2, 1978, Uppsala 1978

Buchholz, H.-G., & Karageorghis, V., Altägäis und Altkypros, Tübingen 1971.

Cadogan, G., "Patterns in the Distribution of Mycenaean Pottery in the Eastern Mediterranean", Acts 1973, 166 ff.

Catling, H., "Cyprus in the Neolithic and Bronze Age Periods", CAH, 3rd revised ed. I-II, 1-2,

Cambridge 1970-71

-----------, "Patterns of Settlement in Bronze Age Cyprus", OpusAth IV, 1963, 129 ff.

Deger-Jalkotzy, S., (ed.) Griechenland, die Ägäis und die Levante während der 'Dark Ages' vom 12. bis zum 9 Jh. v. Chr. Akten des Symposiums von Stift Zwettl (NO) 11-14 Oktober 1980, Vienna 1983

Dikaios, P., "The Excavations at Vounous-Bellapais in Cyprus, 1931-32", Archaeologia 88, 1938, 1 ff.

-----------, Enkomi. Excavations 1948-1958, I-III, Mainz 1969-71.

-----------, & Stewart, J.R., The Stone Age and Early Bronze Age in Cyprus, SCE IV (IA), Lund 1962

Frankel, D., Middle Cypriote White Painted Pottery. An Analytical Study of Decoration (SIMA XLII) Gothenburg

-----------, Early and Middle Bronze Age Material in the Ashmolean Museum, Oxford, (SIMA 20:7) Gothenburg 1983

French, E., & Åström, P., "A Colloquium on LH IIIC Sites", RDAC 1980, 267 ff.

Furumark, A., The Mycenaean Pottery. Analysis and Classification, reprinted Stockholm 1972

Georgiou, H., Relations between Cyprus and the Near East in the Middle and Late Bronze Age, Levant XI, 1979, 84 ff.

Gjerstad, E., Studies on Prehistoric Cyprus, Uppsala 1926

-----------, The Cypro-Geometric, Cypro-Archaic and Cypro-Classical Periods, SCE IV (2), Stockholm 1934-37

-----------, The Phoenician Colonization and expansion in Cyprus" RDAC 1970, 270 ff.

Hankey, V., "Mycenaean Pottery in the Middle East. Notes on Finds since 1951", BSA 62, 1967, 107 ff.

---------, "Aegean Finds at Late Bronze Age Sites in the Southeastern Mediterranean", BICS 19, 143 ff.

---------, "Pottery and People of the Mycenaean IIIC Period in the Levant", Archéologie au Levant: Receuil à la mémoire de Roger Saidah. Collection de la Maison de l'Orient

Méditerranéen 12, Série Archéologique 9, Lyon, 1982, 167 ff.

Harden, D.B., The Phoenicians, London 1962

Iacovou, M., The Pictorial Pottery of Eleventh Century B.C. Cyprus (SIMA LXXIX) Gothenburg 1988

Karageorghis, V., Excavations in the Necropolis of Salamis, I-IV, Nicosia 1967, 1970, 1973 and 1978

----------------, Excavations at Kition, I-III, Nicosia, 1974, 1976, 1977

----------------, & des Gagniers, J., La céramique chypriote de style figuré. Âge du fer (1050-500 Av. J.-C.), Rome 1974

----------------, Alaas. A Protogeometric Necropolis in Cyprus, Nicosia 1975

----------------, & Demas, M., "Excavations at Pyla-Kokkinokremos", RDAC 1981, 135 ff.

----------------, Cyprus from the Stone Age to the Romans, London 1982

----------------, & Muhly, J. (eds.) Cyprus at the Close of the Late Bronze Age, Nicosia 1984

----------------, & Demas, M., Excavations at Maa-Palaekastro 1979-1986, Nicosia 1988

Kling, B., Mycenaean IIIC:1b and Related Pottery in Cyprus, (SIMA LXXXVII) Gothenburg 1989

Knapp, B., Copper Production and Divine Protection: Archaeology, Ideology and Social Complexity on Bronze Age Cyprus (SIMA Pocket-book 42), Gothenburg 1986

Maier, F.G., "Excavations at Kouklia, Paleopaphos", RDAC 1967-79

-----------, "New Evidence for the Early Histroy of Paleopaphos", BSA 78, 1983, 229 f.

-----------, "Ausgrabungen in Alt-Paphos. 13. Vorläufiger Bericht: Grabungskampagne 1983 und 1984", AA, 1986, 145 ff.

Merrillees, R.S., The Cypriote Bronze Age Pottery found in Egypt (SIMA XVIII) Lund 1968

----------------, Trade and Transcendence in the Bronze Age Levant, (SIMA XXXIX) Gothenburg 1974

----------------, Introduction to the Bronze Age Archaeology of Cyprus (SIMA Pocket-boook 9) Gothenburg 1978

Monloup, Therese, Les figurines de terre cuites de tradition archaïque, Salamine de Chypre XII, Paris 1984

Niklasson-Sönnerby, K., "Late Cypriot III Shaft Graves: Burial Customs of the Late Bronze Age", Thanatos, Aegaeum 1, 1987

Peltenburg, E., "Ramesside Egypt and Cyprus", Acts 1986, 149 ff.

Russell, P., The Pottery from the Late Cypriot IIC Settlement at Kalavasos-Ayios Dhimitrios, Cyprus: The 1979-1984 Excavations Seasons (Diss.) Ann Arbor 1986

Sandars, N., The Sea Peoples (2nd ed.) London 1982

Schaeffer, C., Enkomi-Alasia I, Paris 1952

Sjöqvist, E., Problems of the Late Cypriote Bronze Age, Stockholm 1940

Stewart, E. & J., Vounous 1937-38, Lund 1950

Stubbings, F., Mycenaean Pottery from the Levant, Cambridge 1951

Tatton-Brown, V., Cyprus B.C. 7000 Years of History, London 1979

Vermeule, E., Toumba tou Skourou. The Mound of Darkness, Boston 1974

------------, & Karageorghis, V., Mycenaean Pictorial Vase-Painting, Cambridge, Mass. 1982

Villa, P., Early and Middle Bronze Age Pottery of the Cesnola Collection in the Stanford University Museum (SIMA XX:1)

Yon, M., Un depôt de sculpture archaïques, Salamine de Chypre V, Paris 1974

Young, J.H., & S.H., Terracotta Figurines from Kourion in Cyprus, Philadelphia 1955

Desert Vision for Cities in the Sands

Reuben G. Bullard

University of Cincinnati

Cincinnati Bible College & Seminary

No other human being in my acquaintance over the years stands out any more clearly than Dr. Nelson Glueck, president of Hebrew Union College-Jewish Institute of Religion as I knew him. He stood in my graduate student mind as one of the giants of archaeology of mid-century. I can still see the cover of Time, December 13, 1963 featuring a face worn by the elements, framed by the elegance of an Arab kafeyeh headdress. My first physical contact with him was an occasion at Wilson Auditorium, University of Cincinnati campus, where he spoke to students interested in archaeology and specifically his area of research and expertise:Israel, Jordan and the Negev. He spoke quite unlike most men, having a penetrating stare in his eyes as he detailed the great joy he derived from his historical quest by means of field archaeological survey and excavation.

Nelson Glueck was born of a family which had come to Cincinnati from Lithuania on June 4, 1900. Ellen Stern relates a story about Nelson as an eight-year-old boy lingering with his father near Indian mounds at the edge of Cincinnati where he had uncovered a pink quartz arrowhead for his collection. Even at this early age the great mysteries of the past which were held captive by the earth evoked from his curious mind thoughts of the people whose arrowhead he had found. He would ask Papa what those people were like who had carved this quartz artifact. How had they lived, and where had they gone? Once his father remarked, "You're like a thirsty sponge, Nelson . . . endlessly curious . . . and I don't have all the answers."

Nelson Glueck's family in the old world been made up of Torah scholars and rabbis. His father Morris had left Lithuania as a youngster to avoid the necessity of most young men living within the domain of the Russian Czar, military service and the Russian army. He adopted a new name-Mosche Yitzechak Revel became Morris Glueck, the last name being a German word which meant "good luck." His father had met a beautiful young girl also from his Lithuanian home district and Morris and Anna were married over there in 1893. They began living in America in a small house on Court Street in the heart of Cincinnati.

Their third child, Nelson, named for the spring month of Nissan [a time of renewal] knew little outside the orthodox teachings of Judaism. The other eight children also came to learn their prayers easily because in such a household it came naturally, "almost like breathing."

The large family of Morris and Anna Glueck never quite had enough money from his income as a customer peddler on the streets of Cincinnati. Nevertheless, the Glueck family life was a happy one which came to a zenith each week at the time of the setting sun on Friday evening when the heartbeat of the Cincinnati Court Street area slowed down from the high pitch of the bargainers in the vendors' and butchers' shops earlier in the day. Even the noise of playing children ceased when it was time for the Orthodox observation of Sabbath laws. The children could smell the aroma of cooking for the special meal, and even before the Sabbath lamp was lighted, Morris Glueck entered a spotlessly tidy home with the best china already set on the table and a welcoming family. Anna would pull her fringed shawl over her head and light candles which she had brought as a little child from the old country and spoke the prayer bringing the peace and joy of the evening of sabbath to their home. Morris lead the family in the sabbath choruses of the meal.

Warm greetings were shared by neighbors on Court Street when the sabbath was over as visitors from the neighborhood paid their respects to one another. Even though there was little money, Morris and Anna Glueck have been described as a truly rich family. He felt pride as he saw his children absorbing the teachings of his profound love of Judaism. All of his sons and daughters sensed this joy as they celebrated the sabbath and the festivals together and with each other.

Nelson Glueck, described by his biographer Ellen Stern as the most studious of all the Glueck children, showed a love of learning and the understanding that hard work and persistence would bring him success. He did not reveal distraction in the midst of a noisy family household and was often found sitting at the kitchen table doing his homework in the midst of a bustling home.

Nelson did not feel drawn to the business world knowing how hard his father had labored for so little. But he and the other children did work at selling newspapers and at after school jobs to help with their needs as they grew older.

Nelson Glueck showed evidence of a love of study. Would this possibly include becoming a rabbi like his uncle in New York? From time to time Nelson revealed his personal thoughts about his future with his father whom he often found reading by the light of sabbath candles. He told Morris that he held a great admiration for his uncle Rabbi Bernard, but he confessed that he also wanted to study history and science. Morris asked him, "They're good subjects, but why does a rabbi need science?" Nelson replied that he would not be content as a rabbi because he could not enjoy going to school where he was told he couldn't study a subject because it wasn't proper for a pious Jew to learn about it. His father sensed his sons intense desire for learning and that there was something different about this son. Morris said, "Your mother and I have talked about it, and we have decided the training at Hebrew Union College may suit you best." This suggestion revealed that Morris Glueck felt a broad tolerance as an Orthodox Jew, suggesting that his son attend a Reform school which might have advantages over a yeshiva. Nelson Glueck began his education at the Hebrew Union College on Clifton

Avenue in Cincinnati in 1915. It was a school opened by Rabbi Isaac Mayor Wise. This reform movement arose from political changes in the status of American Jews and through the effect of new physical sciences through which Biblical teachings were viewed in a critical, analytical fashion. The impact of modern science on Biblical criticism resulted, in the case of Reform Judaism, in the belief that the Bible, though not physically written by the hand of God, was still the repository of divine ideas which served as man's greatest source of inspiration and instruction. Rabbi Wise, along with others, sought the union of a new kind of Jew with a new kind of frontier America world. The result was the establishment of a Cincinnati Rabbinical Seminary.

Nelson Glueck found favor in the eyes of his teachers at the college where he spent much time studying in the library after his work there in the evenings. His world was now that of discovery and learning. Upon the occasion of his less frequent visits home he heard the frequent talk about the fate of East European Jews and the forces which finally engulfed the world in the First Great War.

There was little question about those aspects of his studies at the college which interested Nelson Glueck most. He often stood in front of the large map of the Holy Land in Professor Deutsch's office and found himself sometimes tracing the outline of those Biblical kingdoms of Edom, Moab, Ammon, and Gilead. During his three years at Hebrew Union College Nelson found an intense interest in the Bible and its text showing the relationship between man and God. The historical facts of the stories absorbed him deeply. His studies came to fruition in 1918 when all of the Glueck family gathered with pride to see their son receive his Bachelor of Hebrew Literature degree at the College. But this was only the first step in his quest and hunger for understanding the past.

The University of Cincinnati was practically across the street, Clifton Avenue, from Hebrew Union College. Here young Glueck enrolled in a series of studies which opened the science of archaeology to him. Unlike researchers guided by precise methods of historical investigation, men previously were driven by a quest for treasures of gold, sculptures, or finds which satisfied the appetites of museum buyers or private collectors. Glueck learned to seek out a different treasure, that which could fill out the unwritten pages of history.

Famous Cincinnati classical and Bronze Age archaeologist, Professor Carl Blegen, was the renown director of the archaeological expeditions of the University of Cincinnati, Classics Department, in Greece and Turkey. His excavations of Bronze Age sites, for example at Pylos and at Troy, yielded the identification of civilizations through artifacts found beneath the site sediments. Known for his expertise in Greek archaeology and for his specialty in the exploration of legendary Troy, he attracted numerous students who have continued his contributions to the archaeological tradition of Cincinnati: Nelson Glueck and John Caskey. Henrich Schliemann's pursuit of the legendary and historical in the Mound of Hissarlik stirred in Nelson Glueck a yearning for the archaeological mode of historical study. This remained strong in his mind through the remainder of his classes at U. C. and stayed with him even as he returned to the halls of Hebrew Union College as a rabbinical student. He achieved his goal in this third chapter of his student life when he stood before Dr. Morgenstern in the chapel of Hebrew Union College and through the "laying on of hands" became "Rabbi Glueck."

Nelson and two other young Americans left home in the fall of 1923 for advanced study in Germany. Here the lifestyle of a German student tempted him but the voice of conscience dictated otherwise. His mentor, Jacob Marcus, saw to it that he and the young men would pursue their real educational objectives. At the University of Berlin Nelson attended classes on the history, culture and civilizations of Palestine. The next year he left for Heidelberg and under the tutelage of the famous scholar, Professor Willi Staerk, pursued work on the background of Biblical writings. His knowledge of German, learned in Cincinnati, was a blessing to him since nearly all the scientific research material was written in that language.

The University of Jena became the third European site of study for him. Here he would write his doctoral dissertation, "The Word 'Grace' in Old Testament Usage," [Hesed], which was accepted by the University in 1927 for his PhD. This work was highly regarded and has been published in more than one language.

Compelled by a motive stated in his own words,
I felt it necessary to learn more about the lands in which the Bible had its roots and about the civilizations and peoples reflected in its pages than was possible to ascertain from extant literature. The only additional source of information was literally in the soil in the Holy Land and of neighboring countries, and the only way to obtain it was, using the modern colloquialism, to dig it.

Nelson Glueck arrived in Jerusalem in Autumn of 1927 and immediately fell in love with the City of David. This affection would drive all of the research throughout the rest of his life.

Shortly, Glueck made his way to the American School of Oriental Research just two blocks north and outside of the Turkish walls of the Old City of Jerusalem. There he met William Foxwell Albright who would become his mentor in field research and ceramic typology through the next three years. It was Dr. Albright who had constructed a new method of analyzing and classifying pottery. A system based upon the shape or morphology of the vessels and their fragments, it became a "highly accurate code" which provided field dating for new finds and the artifacts stratified with them. Even materials from past excavations could be dated more precisely with this method. Palestine is famous for the numerous mounds called Tells which contain ceramic evidence of the stratified times of occupations deposited therein by the building and destruction cycles which characterized these sites through time. For Nelson Glueck, pottery, a near universal packaging medium of antiquity, became one of the principal keys to the past.

From the time Near East people first contained their substances of life in vessels of earthenware, molded of clay and fired in intense heat-jugs for bringing water from wells, bowls for cooking food, jars to store them again in the future-pottery has accompanied them throughout the ages. This same pottery has provided a relatively accurate key to the archaeologist searching out the past [Stern, 1980, p.31]. A competent field archaeologist with the training of W. F. Albright could closely approximate the place and time in which the pottery arose. All this was based upon the assumption that each time frame had its own style of pottery morphology, mostly unique to it alone. His ability to match pottery to items with a positively fixed date, anchored by records of Egyptian kings, queens, or inscription, yielded an accurate reference system. Thus sherds from the rim, base, handle or decorated body styles were analyzed with this index and assembled in a highly documented network procedure.

No doubt was in the mind of Nelson Glueck that Dr. Albright's methodology was superior to anything else available at that time. He took up an assignment as an apprentice to W.F. Albright and his major excavation at Tell Beit Mirsim, a site a little west of Hebron. This expedition introduced Nelson Glueck to the rigors of field archaeology, the daily work schedule of which ranged from 4:15 a. m. to 9:00 p. m. with time for meals, breaks, and lectures interspersed. The site of an ancient Israelite walled town that had seen existence of nearly continuous human occupation from the 13th to the 5th Century B. C., Tell Beit Mirsim, became a model reference site for many Biblical scholars. They believed it to be the town site of Biblical Debir, which was attacked by Joshua in the Hebrew conquest of Canaan. Nelson's tenure with Dr. Albright at this site continued through three years.

The important lesson of staffing a field research expedition was gained by Glueck there. The functioning of the chief archaeologist, architects and photographer, all became the model for that which he would need to know in the future.

After the first year of work with Albright, Nelson Glueck returned home to Cincinnati to a joyous reception. The family house, now in Avondale, was the scene of a joyous occasion. Through smiles and questions he lived his intriguing research in Palestine all over again. His mother's eyes did not leave him. How handsome he was, his dark eyes and thick eyebrows framing those deep expressive eyes, the mobile features tanned by the Palestinian sun. He had missed all of his family during the last five years, and this was a very special time for him. His mother began to ask whether or not it was time for him to get married. The President of Hebrew Union College, Dr. Morganstern, took advantage of the assets he saw in Nelson Glueck and since there would be an opening for instructor at the college, he asked Nelson to fill it. As he stood before this new generation of students, taking his job seriously, those young men could not misread the expression on his face and in his eyes when he spoke to them about the Holy Land. They saw a virtual transformation which came over him as he spoke to them about the hills and wildernesses where "divine purposes had been revealed." Shortly thereafter Nelson Glueck asked for Hebrew Union College to grant him a leave of absence, and he returned to Jerusalem. He began to explore opportunities with Dr. Albright about explorations in Transjordan.

In 1930 Nelson Glueck returned to Cincinnati to resume teaching at the college. Dr. Morganstern was especially proud of the progress that Nelson was making. At this time the school librarian, Mr. Oko introduced Nelson to a girl that would become his wife. She was Helen Iglauer who, after meeting Nelson, returned to her home in Cincinnati's Clifton neighborhood and said to her mother:

"Today I met the most handsome man I've ever seen." She was a sophomore at the University of Cincinnati's Medical School, and was to become the third doctor in her family of German immigrants. Helen's home at 162 Glenmary Avenue, Cincinnati, became a fond refuge for Nelson and after their marriage in 1931, their home.

Scarcely six weeks after the wedding, Nelson returned to dig at Tell Beit Mirsim with Dr. Albright.

Under the auspices of the American School of Oriental Research, Jerusalem, Nelson Glueck's first extensive exploration of the Transjordan began in December 1932. He was accompanied by his young bride, Helen, and several specialists who worked for the Department of Antiquities of Transjordan. Mafraq was the starting point of this expedition and it's exploration since it was conveniently astride the abandoned tracks of the Transjordanian Railway which ran parallel to the boundaries of that country.

His exploration took him south where he found a number of castles, with their intriguing water systems. Elsewhere as they rode southward along the desert route, they observed villages which could offer them no water. He saw that the women from these encampments would take their jugs to springs outside the towns for the needs of their families. He found it incredible that no one of them had thought of cleaning and reusing the ancient cisterns by which they passed.

He observed that the desert Bedouins still moved over trails that had been used through the years. Continuing his research on this expedition and added to it observations from a later aerial flight over this territory, Nelson Glueck found that these tracks indeed had a history.

Centuries and millennia before, the same lines of roadways were already in use because of practically the same geographical, topographical, and economic reasons.

When the messengers of Moses came from Qadesh-Barnea to the kings of Edom and Moab, they promised them that the Israelites would hew through the line of the "King's Highway," the royal road turning neither to the right nor to the left of it. And paying for whatever they obtained in food and drink. What is this "King's Highway" which cut through central Transjordan as early as the time of Moses?Where did this "Royal Road" lead to? . . . It is nothing more and nothing less than the same highway or the line of that highway which in due course of time became Trajan's Road and which today has become Emir Abdullah's Road. The King's Highway led to Aqabaha to Syria.

This intense curiosity for the features of the desert, its sites, its people, their water supplies and courses, their agriculture and their highways became the central thrust of his research through the rest of Nelson Glueck's life.

The love that Dr. Glueck showed for the land of his ancestors as he walked, rode and flew over it making observations and records, drove him through the years. There is no question about his physical stamina and his amazing powers of endurance. The determination that drove him indeed has become proverbial. He was a master of both spoken Hebrew and Arabic and showed a deep sympathy and emotional feeling for all Arab peoples with whom he was associated through the years.

Helen Glueck returned to the United States while Nelson continued his Palestinian research and she pursued her career in medicine back in Cincinnati. He did not want to deprive her of that which was the contribution of her family:medicine. Later, their son Charles would become the fourth in the generation of medical researchers in her side of the family.

The explorations of Nelson Glueck continued until 1937, during which time he was on leave from Hebrew Union College in Cincinnati. In spite of the beginning of a horrible catastrophe in the history of the Jewish people beginning in Europe in 1933, the endless miles of the Transjordanian desert drew Nelson

Glueck on. He adopted the Arab Bedouin way of life and lived with an Arab companion, Ali Abu Ghosh and a camel boy who attended the pack animals carrying their camping and research equipment. The camel was his vehicle.

He quickly learned the etiquette of the desert and the necessity of inquiring from the local sheik or chieftain about the territory under his care. Legendary Arab hospitality was offered him not only in the company of heavily armed men, but also in their tents. Drink and food were served in a manner of amazing friendliness that reaches back to the time of Abraham. All this was but the introduction to any opportunity he hoped to achieve in his studies.

Nevertheless, food to which he was unaccustomed along with parasites both external and internal took hold of him and were a part of his life for the years he spent in the desert. I was told that he had to be "dewormed" upon his return to the United States after this phase of his research was completed in 1947.

The lessons of desert etiquette were well learned by Nelson Glueck who was granted the freedom to roam the area. The guards provided by his hosts guided him to sites which he wanted to study while they protected him from enemy tribes.

In a manner somewhat similar to that of Lawrence of Arabia, Nelson Glueck put on Bedouin robes and rode camels. The thrust of the former was military and political, certainly not without sympathies for the Arab people, while the quest of the latter was historic and Biblical. Neither heat nor flies nor dust nor sand which were ever-present kept him from these noble objectives.

I have never looked east towards the hills of Moab without being seized by a sense of excitement. I have never yet started climbing steeply towards their tops without wondering what new mystery would reveal itself to me. For these lands east, as well as the Jordan, are haunted by the shades of history and throb with the pulse of the past. These are more than conglomerations of rock and soil, with springs and plants, animals and people. These are the haunts of the children of God, and his spirit is imprinted in the very atmosphere. I have stood on the shores of the Red Sea and heard the accents of Jehovah in Sinai. I have wandered in the wastes of the desert and heard the weeping of Hagar. I have sat in the tents of Ishmael and found myself peering into the faces of prophets. I have paced along the banks of the Jordan and watched the people of Israel crossing over into the promised land.

Old Testament passages were studied in connection with the potsherds found at the places they describe. Nelson Glueck the scholar/archaeologist had the soul of a poet and, beyond question, the desert was that place where the past became alive in the present for him.

His research in Transjordan continued during the summers from 1932 until 1946 during which time he explored much of the territory systematically. The results were published as "Explorations in Eastern Palestine" in the Bulletin for the American Schools of Oriental Research.

World War II presented a chapter of a totally different subject matter to the scholar/explorer. He had been approached by Colonel William Donovan of the American Office of Strategic Services in Washington. Would Nelson Glueck assist the Allies in locating possible retreat routes for the British army in North Africa should Rommel and the Germans win the inevitable and fateful battle which would eventually culminate there. Although he has been characterized as a spy by some, this function of the field archaeologist was in the service of his country and for the emergency purposes of saving the lives of soldiers in a possible retreat. In my view there is nothing about his service in this capacity which had any negative relationship to the Arab community or its local or national government.

The first American-born president of Hebrew University in Jerusalem, Palestine, was Rabbi Judah L. Magnes. He was a strong proponent of a Jewish home in Palestine and had left a prominent career in the United States as an educator and clergyman to come to the Near East in the 1920s. He worked on behalf of peace following World War I in Europe and took part in more relief programs there. Among those dedicated men who sought to build up an institution of higher learning in Jerusalem, he was one of the founders who dedicated the Hebrew University campus on Mt. Scopus to the northeast of the Old City. He was a prominent mentor in the life of Nelson Glueck during the crisis hours of the beginning of the conflict among the British patrols and against Jews endeavoring to come to the area of Palestine after having fled the horrors of Hitler's initial policies in Germany and Poland.

Rabbi Magnes continued to encourage Nelson Glueck in his work with the American School noting especially that his historical research gave a special consciousness to those who sought their roots on this soil. He also mentioned that there was an enormous job of uniting the American Jewish community behind that which would someday take place in Palestine on behalf of the Jews of the world.

Helen and the baby Charles Glueck had already returned to Cincinnati when Nelson decided also to leave in August of 1940. Westward movement through the Mediterranean by ship was no longer possible so he took an eastern route to Baghdad and Basra where he got steamer passage down the Persian Gulf to Pakistan, India, South Africa, and finally to New York City. The Second Great War of the world was in progress in Europe and there were massive flights of people from the German army everywhere. Soon after his arrival in their Clifton home in Cincinnati, Nelson heard the footsteps of Helen rapidly coming upstairs to his study where with a pale and shocked face she said, "Nelson, Pearl Harbor has just been bombed by the Japanese!"

Soon thereafter he returned to Palestine and assumed the direction of the American School in Jerusalem and accepted the role of Field Director of the Baghdad branch of the American Schools of Oriental Research also. Most of the archaeological work of the Middle East had ceased because of the war and many of his associates had been recalled to serve in the conflict. He was nearly alone in the field now. As he roamed the desert again in the quest of ancient sites which he recorded on his nearly empty map, he associated with Arab encampments and received their well-known hospitality. His association was not only with Sheiks but also with poor tribesmen whom he respected and enjoyed alike. As mentioned earlier, Nelson Glueck was not in any sense a traditional spy. He listened carefully to discussions about the movements of strangers in the desert and noted that one of those groups of visitors could only be German spies operating in the area. His intelligence assignment was information concerning retreat routes for Allied soldiers and under no circumstances did he seek to betray any of his Arab hosts. He even possessed a special code by which he could transmit to Washington information that would assist the Allies in the determination of their actions against Germans.

All the while he was helping to build a foundation for the study of human civilization in this portion of the Fertile Crescent. Each time he returned to Jerusalem from his field work, disturbing news of the present greeted him. One after another, the Jewish communities of Poland, Russia, France, Belgium, Romania, and Greece were destroyed by the German onslaught. The real facts of Jewish suffering had not yet come to the outside world, but Nelson Glueck as a Jew and a Rabbi grieved over these people, the descendants of Abraham and Moses, as he learned of the destruction of their places of worship and learning in Europe.

The fruit of these tenuous research years in Palestine came with the publication of the amazing knowledge of Biblical and historical information as The River Jordan in 1946. As the consciousness of the enormous European Holocaust came to Nelson Glueck in Jerusalem, he was preparing to leave Jerusalem for a return to his position at Hebrew Union College in Cincinnati. It was a time of tension and terrorism in Palestine because Arab hostilities, which had begun in the late 30's, were being renewed. As he was preparing for departure, a letter came from Cincinnati which would alter his life's direction:"Would he consider the presidency of Hebrew Union College?"

In 1947 he accepted a little reluctantly the presidency of the Cincinnati institution even though the call of the desert remained strong in his heart. The insistent persuasion of Rabbi Magnes convinced him to accept the position which drew his maximum attention with vigor and excitement. In 1950 Stephen Wise urged him to assume the responsibility of leadership for the Jewish Institute of Religion in New York and he became the president of the combined colleges. Soon these rabbinical schools opened a third institution in Los Angeles and in 1963 Nelson Glueck opened one mainly of his own creation in Jerusalem--the Biblical and Archaeological School of the Hebrew Union College-Jewish Institution of Religion in Jerusalem.

Ellen Norman Stern said that Nelson Glueck believed the American Jewish community was not sufficiently cognizant of its own background and history. He encouraged Dr. Jacob Marcus, a faculty member of the Cincinnati Institute, to create a national archives on the campus of Hebrew Union College which would become a treasure house for students of American Jewish history. It became the largest collection of Jewish historical material in the United States and is being widely used by students of all denominations in their research.

In 1947 and 1948 the evacuation of the British forces from mandated Palestine, gave rise to the war of the Jews and Arabs and the partitioning of this land. After this time Nelson Glueck would not be admitted under any circumstances by the Arabs to the territories under the control of the Hashmenite Kingdom of Jordan. He was not even allowed to return to the American School north of the Old City of Jerusalem.

Nelson Glueck had waited with impatience to return to Palestine/Israel, the latter having gained its independence and its long-dreamed-of homeland. In 1948 he assumed a close association with the first prime minister of Israel, David Ben-Gurion, at his Negev kibutz home, Sde Boker, south of Beersheba. Ben-Gurion noted that most of Israel's territory was desert and wilderness although its population was situated mainly in cities. This clustering appeared unwise to him. "We need a lifeline through the Negev like King Solomon had from Beersheba to the Red Sea. I would like to see a string of towns built in the desert from here to the Gulf of Acaba as he pointed southward. "

This conversation initiated a program by Nelson Glueck to explore that which he had not completed before when he extended his work in the Transjordan down into the Araba and along the western margins of the Negev. Now he could explore with the blessings of the new state the territory of this so-called desert in the southern part of Israel. Tensions in the area had prevented Glueck from mounting any new major projects since his work in connection with the Transjordanian territory. Deploring these constrictions upon him, he was now eager to resume the work of his Transjordanian survey in the desert from Aqaba to Beersheba, seeking out the traces of its history.

He acted in contradiction to the common assumption that the environmental climate had altered this area so measurably that neither man or beast could exist there in any other context than that of the Bedouin, those nomads who eternally wandered in pursuit of water and food for their families and flocks.

There was little doubt in the mind of Nelson Glueck about the importance of the Negev, both for the ancient history of the land and for the new nation. Now all of the sensitivity, techniques, and desert acumen he had learned in Transjordan would be employed in the desert of the south. The immediate value and results of his work would be the colonization by young Israelis in this foreboding land. This would be a new kind of experience for him. The territory of the new state of Israel was now less secure and safe than ever for any explorer to search out the lands of the Bible. Arab snipers and terrorists made it impossible for him to travel alone so a small party of the Israeli army soldiers traveled with him.

The enthusiasm of Nelson Glueck soon rubbed off on those young soldiers whose fascination for the great reconstruction of their own history matched his own. The mode of travel now would be no longer camels but jeeps which would not only shorten travel time but also carry the military equipment for security and for calling in help. The United States Army gave him a command car, which was in use into the late 1960's. I drove it in my field reconnaissance at Tell Gezer.

This second phase of his research brought Nelson Glueck to stirring conclusions. Never before had the full spectrum of resources, personal dreams and intuitions been brought together in such a way as to combine the quest for ancient history knowledge and its technology which could provide long lost insights into overcoming and conquering the desert for the new nation's aspiring people.

The modus operandi of Dr. Glueck was, beyond question, the Biblical accounts and the pottery typology which he had mastered with W. F. Albright earlier. He saw in these seemingly barren wastelands an historical memory of the Bible and did not regard the Negev as a true desert. He realized that it had been inhabited from time to time through history and felt that no other place on the planet had played so important an historical role for engendering ideas. The region of the Negev and Sinai had been studied as the geography of well known portions of Biblical history which had strongly influenced the lives of Abraham and Moses. Oftentimes, Glueck was seared there by the sun and desiccated by dry winds and dust. He found archaeological contexts scarred by the shocking evidence of child sacrifice which brought to life in his mind the substitution of a ram for his own son Isaac in the history of the Abraham, the Father of the Hebrews. Glueck saw this superstition and pagan religious concept shattered by Abraham, who in his moment of refusal to participate in the sacrificial worship of his time brought about a change of everlasting importance. "Never again would the people of Abraham be like the neighboring tribes of the desert. While all around them others played to many gods, Abraham and his followers worshiped the One God who had commanded them to save a human life and serve Him in righteousness. This would be the core of their religion forever." As a summary statement of his experiences in this blazing land, Nelson Glueck entitled his chapter on the area, "Heart Land of Conscience" in his book River in the Desert. The explorations of the Negev by Nelson Glueck in the 1950s inspired the founding of new cities by Israeli colonists in that desert from Beersheba to Eilat on the Gulf of Aqaba.

After he had completed his desert research, he embarked upon another phase in his life. John F. Kennedy had asked President Glueck to participate in his inauguration early in January of 1961. Along with the poet Robert Frost, President Glueck participated in the ceremonies on the podium and then at the appointed moment stepped in front of cabinet officers and ex-presidents and prayed, "May the Lord bless thee and keep thee, May the Lord make his face to shine upon thee and be gracious unto thee, May the Lord lift up His countenance and give thee peace." In ancient Biblical words of sanctification, the head of Hebrew Union College-Jewish Institute of Religion, launched the Kennedy administration.

The writings of Nelson Glueck appeared different from any others that were involved with the subject of Biblical research. In a gripping way he added his own emotional and spiritual feelings to his words which gave them a popular appeal although

> he had never intended any of his scientific work to "prove" the accuracy of the Bible, but then found that most of his archaeological discoveries bore out the amazing literal truth in the Bible.

Something very special was to happen in the life of the man who loved the history of this ancient land so much. Hebrew Union College's School of

Archaeology was inaugurated in Jerusalem in July of 1963, praised by both the government of Israel and Jewish Agency members. The location awarded Glueck for the school's place of honor in the city was 13 King David Street, not far from the King David Hotel and the YMCA. This institutional beginning was engendered by the fact that the American School of Oriental Research was cut off from the Jewish side of the city by a no man's land that would permit no Jew to pass. It was another of Nelson's fondest dreams come true. Prime Minister Ben-Gurion, Abba Eban, Moshe Sharett, Golda Meir and the President of Israel, Yitzak Ben-Zbi were among the many who took part in the festive activities which took place in the new school's white Galilean limestone building.

Before this auspicious event, Nelson stood on the spot where the foundations of the building were being laid and watched the workman fulfilling his dream, a shot was fired at him not unlike the times that the Arab nomads expressed their displeasure at his appearance at their desert water-holes. But this time was different. Members of the Orthodox Religious parties had expressed strong feelings against giving the land for this school and its synagogue to the American Reform movement. It was, however, declared by the prime minister that the Israeli constitution granted freedom to all religions. During its opening service, the beautiful Oriental tonalities of the Sephardic liturgical music treasures were selected by Glueck. He saw this as a blending of the ancient with the modern even as this inspiring new school had arisen on an hilly street in West Jerusalem within site of the Java gate of the Old City's western walls. This service is inspiringly described by Ellen Stern:

> Nelson's face glowed. The clear, silvery sounds of the flute, the warm velvety tune of the cello accompanied the words sung by the cantor and the female choir. And the words found their echoes in Nelson's heart, "Let everything that hath breath praise the Lord. Hallelujah. "

The last major accomplishment of this extraordinary man was the fulfillment of another dream which united his effort with that of Dr. George Ernest Wright of Harvard University. He and his students joined the Hebrew Union College-Jewish Institute of Religion's School of Archaeology as co-sponsor of a dig at Tell Gezer which Wright felt was important since its excavator just after the turn of the century, R. A. S. MacCalister, had not utilized stratigraphic principals in the digging of the mound in the foothills half way between Jerusalem and Tel Aviv. This excavation under the careful eyes of both advisors, Wright and Glueck, would add a new dimension to Near Eastern, especially Biblical archaeology: trained scientists would be a part of its core staff.

A final accolade came in October of 1964 back in Cincinnati. The College/Institute was celebrating Nelson Glueck's 20th anniversary as its president with a grand banquet at Cincinnati's Netherland Hilton Hotel. Featured speaker was his former teacher and mentor, Dr. William F. Albright. In a speech which carried the title "A Hero of Biblical Archaeology" great praise was accorded to his former student whom he praised for his mastery of Palestinian pottery morphology and his research, eagerly shared by Jews and Christians, which sought to reconstruct the historical background of their religious faith.

Nelson Glueck resigned as president of Hebrew Union College-Jewish Institution in 1969 to retire. His successor, Rabbi Alfred Gottschalk, head of the California branch of the schools, would, in a short time, characterize Nelson Glueck in his eulogy as a fierce champion for Jewish dignity and survival. "A son of Jerusalem and of Cincinnati, was drawn to the land of his ethnic and spiritual fathers by an uncommon mystic vision. "He continued that Glueck was the great guiding spirit for the rabbinical schools whose presidency was characterized with brilliance, imagination, and tireless zeal. He had attracted funds as no other for the growth of these institutions both in American and in Jerusalem. "Let us continue to

build on his dreams, grow on his imagination, enlarge his work, preserve his vision
. . . . amen".

Thus Nelson Glueck died in Cincinnati after a short illness on 12 February
1971. Once in an article in the <u>American Jewish Yearbook</u>, Nelson Glueck's
religious views were described as "naive. "This label is clearly unfitting. As one
may never fully know the thoughts that we have, his own words from <u>The River</u>
<u>Jordan</u> concerning Mount Nebo are far from the direction of any naivety.

All this, and more too, is what Moses "man of God" (Psalm 90:1) saw
as he stood alone on the summit of the mountain--alone, except for the
companionship and call of the God whom he had never forsaken and
silent before this manifestation of another of the Lord's miracles. At
least, the realization of a generation's striving the accomplishment of
an agony of effort, the fulfillment of driving dreams for freedom!But
not for you, O' Moses, your work is done. For you, this is journey's
end. The stream of your life is entering into the sea of death.

Selected Facets of Nelson Glueck's Research Career

Dr. John L. Caskey, Professor of Classical Archaeology, University of Cincinnati was nearly a contemporary of Nelson Glueck. He wrote in the Yearbook for 1972 of the American Philosophical Society, that Glueck's character, which if it could be described, was marked by "integrity, industry, generosity, and humility, combined with enthusiasm, sensitivity, and warm emotions." I would like to present a piece of personal history and interaction with Nelson Glueck along with my analysis of his field research perceptions in his work through the years.

An amazing and magnanimous event highlighted Dr. Nelson Glueck's actions as president of HUC-JIR in 1963. As this writer was seeking to discover opportunities by which geological research methods could be applied to archaeological field excavations, he made an appointment with the president on December 23, 1963 at the Clifton Avenue campus. At 1:30 p. m. he was welcomed into the Klau Library office where he was warmly greeted. Dr. Glueck said, "How may I help you?" Appreciating his immediate directness, I said, "Dr. Glueck, I am a PhD. track student in the University of Cincinnati Geology Department and I am casting about to determine the focus of my research. I want to apply scientific techniques of a geological nature to archaeological sites and their environments. "His eyes began flashing warmly under those very dense eyebrows and I had scarcely spoken the last word when he burst out with, "Ah! If you had been here two years ago you could have gone with me to the Negev!" He opened his desk drawer and took out a pad asking, "How much will you need? Will your wife want to go also?"

This was the beginning of seven years of research at Tell Gezer in the Shephelah of Israel, where I was appointed to the position of staff geologist. This was a first in the expansion of the activities of Biblical archaeological field work to include scientific/environmental studies. Nelson Glueck had shown a unique [the same request had been turned down by another famous archaeologist] and direct interest in the implementation of new scientific ideas and methods at the site sponsored by both Hebrew Union College and Harvard. My wife and I both saw him at the excavation where he came to visit and, at times, to speak. Lynn held him in the highest regard both for his remarks to her as she helped with the pottery washing at the site and in the Glueck home in Clifton when we were dinner guests. He wanted her to sit beside him during the meal.

After I had made contact with Nelson Glueck in this fruitful interview, he soon asked me to help him with research on his copper smelting studies from the Araba and neighboring plateau lands. By this he showed the broadest sense of historical responsibility to his opportunities of presenting the best possible field research results. The outcome of my research is presented below.

Another special incident occurred one time very soon after the end of the Six Day War, June 1967. He drove three of us from the Gezer staff up onto the newly won Golan Heights. We saw unexploded bombs still standing in the fields where they had fallen and ammunition scattered all along the side of the road. He was so excited and intensely interested in the sights that he was experiencing in this area from which he had been forbidden for more than 20 years that he failed to realize, along with the rest of us, that he had made a turn that was taking us directly into the Syrian army cease-fire lines. Upon the advice of an Israeli soldier we turned from the area a quarter of a mile of that possibility in which all of us could have become Syrian prisoners, perhaps on a long-term basis!

As I turned to his explicit love and fascination for the desert, Nelson Glueck confirmed the error of George Adams Smith, who had stated a judgment in his historical geography that "no great route now leads or ever has led through the Negev similar to that from Dan to Beersheba, where during the greater part of history, the means of settled civilization came to an end. The Negev was simply regarded as a forbidding and inhospitable desert. Glueck, however, did not view this as a consequence of climate change through time. He said, "Extreme desolation created repeatedly by merciless invaders resulted often in the total disappearance of civilization. "Glueck cited Judges 9:45, "'And he took the city and slew the people that were therein; and he beat down the city and sowed it with salt. 'But the desert has seemed to fool us. When new settlers arrived, sometimes after prolonged intervals of time, they would neither know or be able to recognize the locations of the previous town sites and would build their houses of stone or mud brick on virgin soil. No firmly rooted people of the land would be left to remain and transmit from historical memories the heritage of unbroken traditions." (Rivers in the Desert, p. 6). For him, the long history of the rise and fall of civilizations in the desert of the Transjordan and the Negev with alternating times of sedentary occupation and periods of emptiness stood in contrast to the Bedouin mastery of the land in this century. He concluded therefore that the historical gap must be ascribed to wars and economic blight rather than to drastic changes in weather.

Fully acknowledging his indebtedness to those Arab sheiks who befriended them and their guides who led him in Transjordan and the Araba, he added his gratitude for the young Israeli soldiers who escorted him in a different political world in the Negev. As a result as his personal research drive, he wrote, "A blank space on a historical map is a constant challenge to the explorer and archaeologist. Its emptiness disturbs him. What role, if any, did it play in the development of civilization?Where and when did its ancient inhabitants live. Was it's soil rich or poor, its water plentiful or lacking, its minerals abundant or unknown, its landscape attractive or forbidding, its geographical position of great or indifferent importance?" (Rivers in the Desert, ix, 8.)

Whenever I heard Dr. Glueck speak on the University of Cincinnati campus, or at the site of Tell Gezer in Israel, what I experienced with him

personally was confirmed by his statement of purpose which is framed in these
words.

> I have never travelled through this part of the world without being
> seized by a sense of excitement. I have never wandered about across
> its spaces, knowing that I was treading ground where the Patriarchs
> and the Prophets had lived without wondering what new view of the
> miraculous [sic] might possibly be unrolled before me. I have never
> explored the Negev or Sinai without realizing that in those lands
> God's will was revealed to mortal men giving them the possibility of a
> status lower than the angels. I have never paced up and down the
> banks of the Jordan without in my mind's eye seeing the people of
> Israel cross over into the Promised Land and wondering what the
> spiritual equivalent of the Promised Land might be in our time.
> "[Stern]

In all of this there emerges a clear mystique which, together with his personal
words, always excited the desire to cooperate in his students and colleagues, and,
especially, in me.

A side of Nelson Glueck which is either unknown or has been criticized for
its absence was his concern for the scientific controls in his field excavation
research. The following material illustrates the very strongly contrary reality. As a
scientist I was warmly welcomed and invited to participate in the field research
with which he had been and would be connected. Geological studies were
introduced into Syro-Palestinian field archaeology in 1966, and he made known his
pleasure and satisfaction at this dimension of study at the new excavation
sponsored by his institution and by Harvard. He sought retrospective investigation
for his previous conclusions about his Tell el-Keleifeh material science and
metallurgical studies. He had made judgements there which were received by the
popular press and by historians and Biblical workers with enthusiasm. He lacked,
however, any specific training in the subsciences of sedimentology,
pyrotechnology, and metallurgy. He had simply misstated the function of a large
mud brick building with half-beam impressions in two different levels of its walls.

sponsored by his institution and by Harvard. He sought retrospective investigation for his previous conclusions about his Tell el-Keleifeh material science and metallurgical studies. He had made judgements there which were received by the popular press and by historians and Biblical workers with enthusiasm. He lacked, however, any specific training in the subsciences of sedimentology, pyrotechnology, and metallurgy. He had simply misstated the function of a large mud brick building with half-beam impressions in two different levels of its walls. He assumed it was a large smelter used by Solomon's workman to produce copper. With the help of scientific specialists, he realized that his judgment had been wrong, having called this site of Ezion-Geber, King Solomon's Pittsburg of antiquity. He candidly and generously reversed his views as he noted that...

We had originally thought these apertures served as flue-holes during Period I of the Solomonic Period of this structure which was first considered by us to be an advanced type of smelter-refinery. Through these apertures or flue-holes, we theorized, the strong and steady winds from the north-northwest were led into the furnace rooms of this so-called "smelter" to furnish a natural draft to fan the flames, employing at a very early date the basic principals of the Bessemer blast furnace.

The ability of this man with his fertile mind to reverse himself and publicly revise the conclusions according to the data is boldly set forth in this way:

Further study has, however, now convinced us that these apertures were not intended as flue-holes or as ventilation channels for any related purpose. They resulted from ancient, and to a measure still utilized, building techniques in the construction of mud brick buildings. . . . Examples of this kind of construction mud brick walls

may be observed at sites in Turkey, Crete, and Mesopotamia (The Other Side of the Jordan, p. 111, Et Passim).

This abrupt change in his view was conditioned by his openness to scientific investigations of the very materials from which he had drawn his earlier conclusions. No better example of personal greatness is needed.

Nelson Glueck maintained a conscious effort to embrace the total culture of those peoples whose remains he studied. He was sensitive to the bright green fragments of malachite, a copper mineral composed of an easily smelted carbonate, along the slopes of tributary wadis to the Araba. Of special interest to him were sites at Khirbet Nahas (Copper Ruin) and at Timnah. In these places he confirmed for himself that statement in Deuteronomy 8:9, "Out of whose hills thou canst dig copper. "He additionally noted the small smelting operations from which there were left rings of copper slag along with ceramic evidence for their Iron I date of the time of King Solomon.

There was no barrenness of these desert lands in the mind of Nelson Glueck. He affirmed that he could show us "a thousand or more sites of antiquity in Transjordan which existed during and after the time that the land was supposed no longer to be able to sustain them. "The climate was alleged to be the principal factor.

But there was another side to the Nelson Glueck story. He saw that the problem lay in the fact that most of these ruins which dot the surface could not have been discovered without mastery of "the modern techniques and tools of archaeological investigation." He acknowledged freely that all of this was due to the foundational work of Sir Flinders Petrie, Pre Hugo Vincent, Clarence S. Fisher and William F. Albright. Glueck affirmed that these archaeologists had provided the science of pottery identification with a development "such that from broken fragments alone, nearly universally found on the surface of every ancient site, the competent student should be able to determine the span of the civilized occupation they represent with less an error than a hundred years in a thousand." "Pottery made of clay, mixed with a binding material of tiny stones and shells and baked in a kiln is perhaps the most durable substance man has ever created." (Rivers in the Desert, p. 8). In one of the most evocative statements about surface sherding in connection with an organized surface survey, he affirmed that he had . . .

gathered the pottery from surfaces of one or another ancient site which fairly shout out the periods of history they belong to. It is as if they had been waiting for ages for someone to come along and notice them and pick them up, so that they could describe with eloquent pride the time and quality of their kingdoms. I can assure you that the archaeologists regards each artifact with feelings akin to personal affection. " (Rivers in the Desert, p. 9).

As evidence of the advance of his concepts of research in his day, Nelson Glueck not only used surface techniques of discovery, but he also took advantage of opportunities to observe the desert surface from the air. The delineation of a highway track, the carefully designed and constructed water conservation measures, his acute sense of the presence of ores and slags, his mastery of ceramic typology which he endeavored to correct as the methodology changed during his lifetime, and the amazing vision of the ancient history of the desert areas characterize his amazing qualities, all distinguish a far from naive scholar. I can even yet hear the words made famous in his lectures in which he excitedly affirms

gone are the shouting and smells of the caravans that once halted at Qasr Umm el-Qeseir. The pathway leading past it will, however, always be sought out as long as human beings live and travel in this part of the world. Some of them may be as energetic and creative as the Nabataeans, and others as unwittingly durable as the feckless nomads who tent beside their ruins. Much of the story of the creation of the earth and of the strivings of mankind can be read in the fossil-laden building blocks of this site and in the fragments of fine Nabataean and later pottery that can be found among them. The petrified conglomeration of primeval matter and sea creatures out of which buildings were constructed and the earthenware formed and fired by mortal men bear a relationship to each other that is established in the wonder of the divine order. (Rivers in the Desert, p. 235).

Nelson Glueck also affirmed that he had found evidence for Solomon's use of the Negev as his line of protection and communication between Ezion-Geber and Jerusalem. He stated that our view of history should include archaeology, geography, Biblical credibility and common sense as he insisted upon the certainty of the place of Ezion-Geber in the history of Israel.

The many years of desert research gave him an uncommon sensitivity for the essential presence of water in the environment. He wrote extensively about all aspects of water engineering and husbandry in his study of ancient desert peoples. He did not hesitate to broach the issue of the technical water engineering essential to enable Nabataean and early desert civilizations to survive.

In a brilliant work that summed up much of his research in Transjordan, Nelson Glueck published a valuable treatise on the Nabataeans. With Petra and several other cities and settlements along their mainly traveled routes, "They were rescued from oblivion by employing, on a country-wide scale, the modern 20th Century A. D. tool of identification of surface signs of pottery fragments. As a result, these territories in the hamlets, villages, and towns that once started them were placed within the framework of history." (Deities and Dolphins, p. 536).

Aside from these facets of his approach to archaeological field work, he employed another personal involvement that we only rarely see. He consciously endeavored to view the historical situation he was studying from the framework of those who lived in it.

> ... When we were examining the impressive remains of a very strong fortress that had in all probability been erected under Uzziah's orders, let me relate my impressions as I imagined them at the time in connection with this particular strong hold. I gave myself the role of a member of the chief architect's entourage, awaiting the visit of a royal commission to examine and take over the fortress he had designed and the construction of which he had supervised (The River Jordan, p. 174-5).

Glueck continued through two pages of text to describe in vivid words the visit of the kings overseers to the site over which he, the local builder, was given charge. His description of this scene was almost that of an eyewitness, and indeed, his historical vision was nearly unique, and not unlike that of George Ernest Wright from whom I had heard similar personal historical vision accounts when in his company.

In conclusion it is only fitting for me to relate the outcome of Dr. Nelson Glueck's vision-the same vision he had used in the desert to see the past-to embrace the future. The opening that he gave to geologic studies at archaeological sites, which began in Tell Gezer, was imitated by both Americans and Israelis and others at other sites throughout the Near East. Specialized studies in petrology, sedimentation, topography, hydrogeology, stratigraphy, depositional structures and the development of the concept of archaeo-depo-sites and much more have developed. His quest for the fullest dimension of archaeological research provided one of the bases for the founding of a new unit of the Geological Society of America in 1976: The Archaeological Geology Division, five years after his death. This association has grown to have a membership of 500 scientists-a monument to his perception and that of others.

BIBLIOGRPAHY

"Archaeology: The Shards of History (cover story)." _Time_, December 13, 1963.

Bamberger, Fritz. _The Mind of Nelson Glueck_. Doubleday & Company, Inc., 1970.

Bamberger, Fritz. "Nelson Glueck: 1900-1971 - A Tribute." _The Hour Glass_, Vol IV-Nos. 1-2, 1971.

Bliss, Betty. "He's a Man of All Times." _The [Cincinnati] Enquirer_, 1968.

Caskey, J.L. "The American Philosophical Society." Year Book 1972.

Current Biography. "Nelson Glueck." July 1969.

Dever, William. Personal note. November 18, 1989.

Glueck, Nelson. _Hesed in the Bible_. Cincinnati: The Hebrew Union College Press, 1967.

Glueck, Nelson. _Rivers in the Desert: A History of the Negev_. New York: Farrar, Straus and Cudahy, 1959.

Glueck, Nelson. _Deities and Dolphins_. New York: Farrar, Straus and Giroux, 1965.

Glueck, Nelson. _The River Jordan_. New York: McGraw-Hill Book Company, 1968.

Glueck, Nelson. _The Other Side of the Jordan_. Cambridge, Mass: American Schools of Oriental Research, 1970.

Gottschalk, Alfred. "Nelson Glueck." Cincinnati, (eulogy 1971).

Roseman, Kenneth D. "Words Spoken at Memorial Service for Dr. Nelson Glueck." Cincinnati, 1972.

Stern, Ellen Norman. _Dreamer in the Desert_. New York: KTAV Publishing House, Inc., 1980.

University of Cincinnati. "The Man Who Discovered King Solomon's Mines."

1

2

4

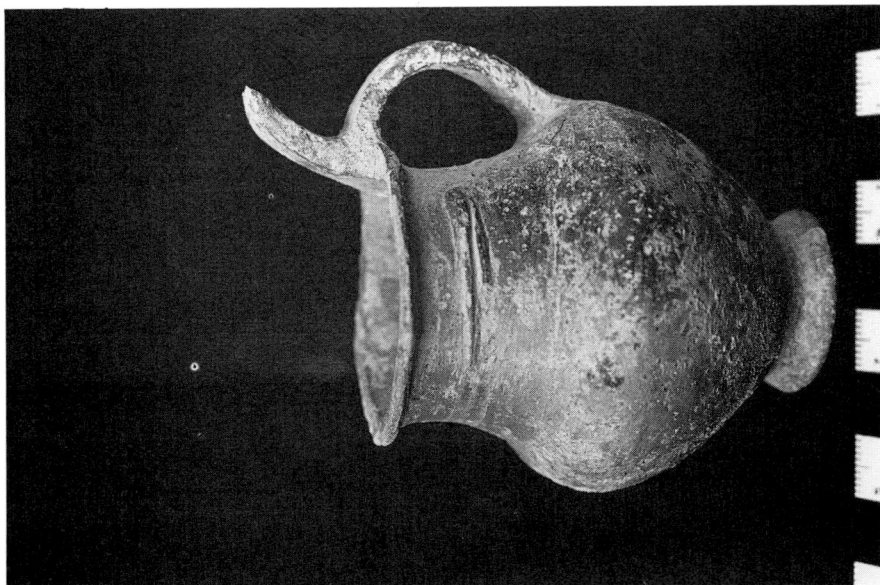

cc

7

10

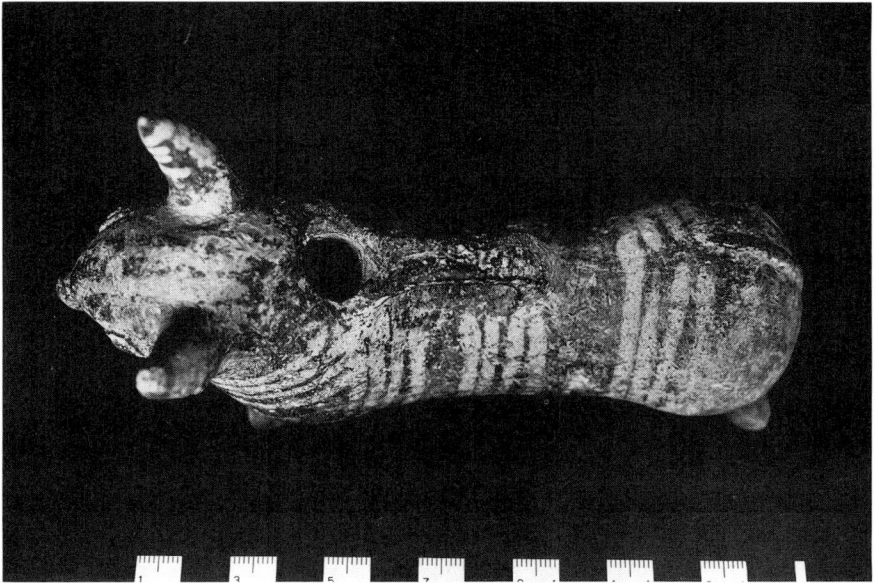

11

12

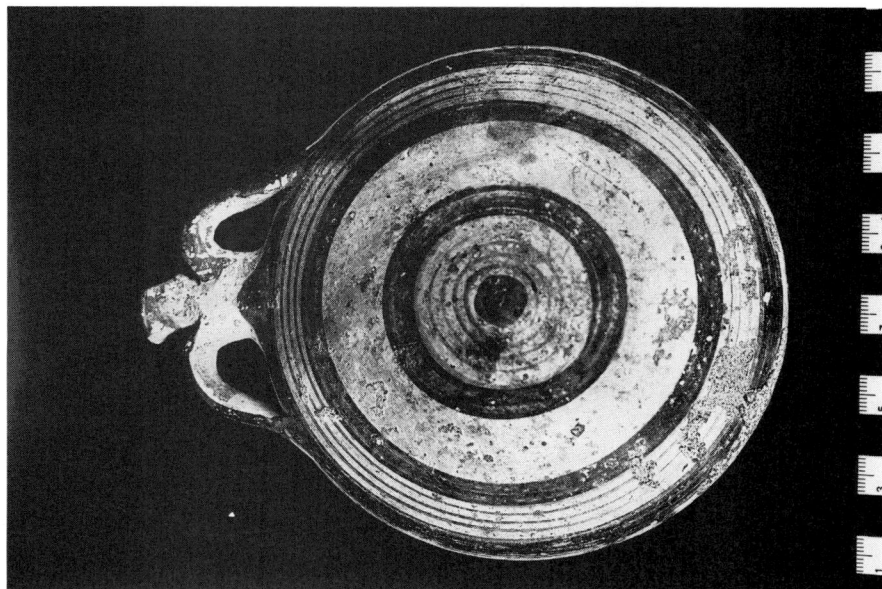

14

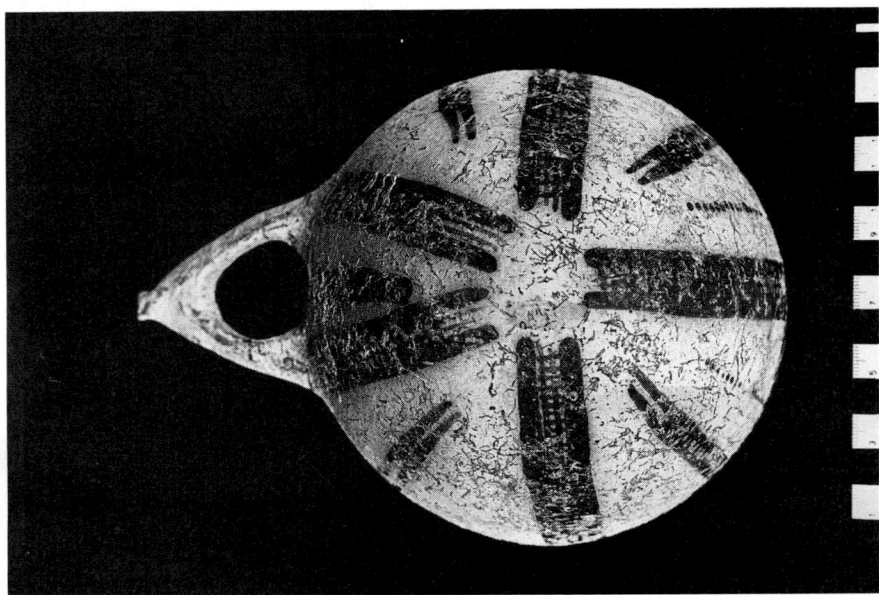

15

18

17

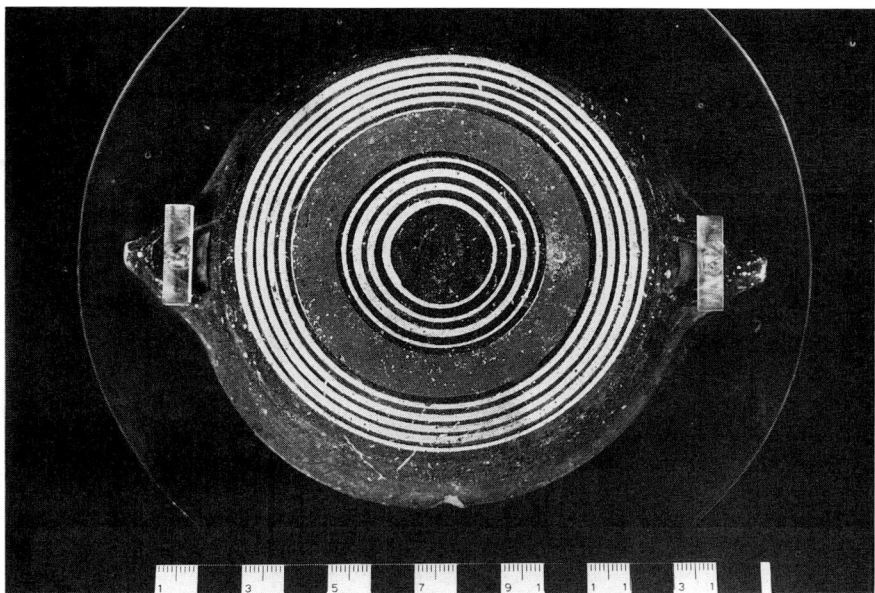

21

23

22

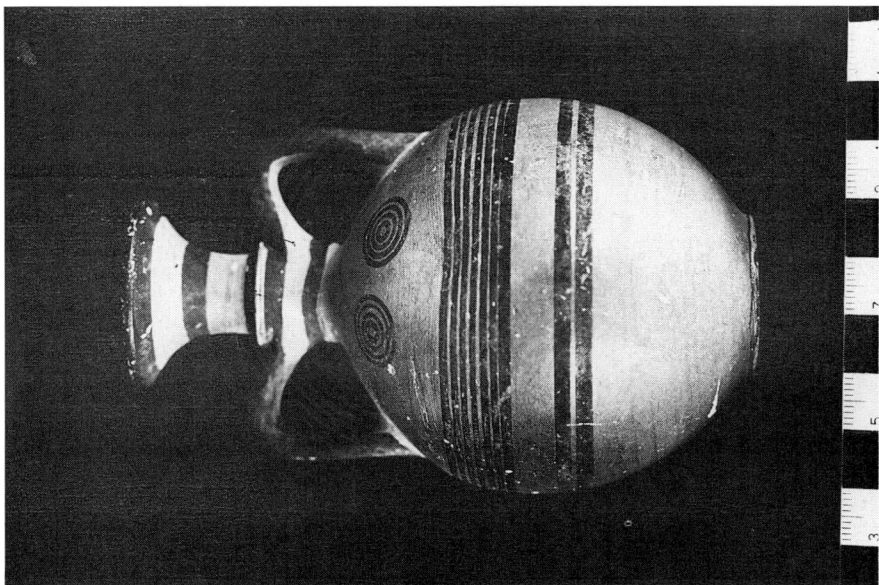

24

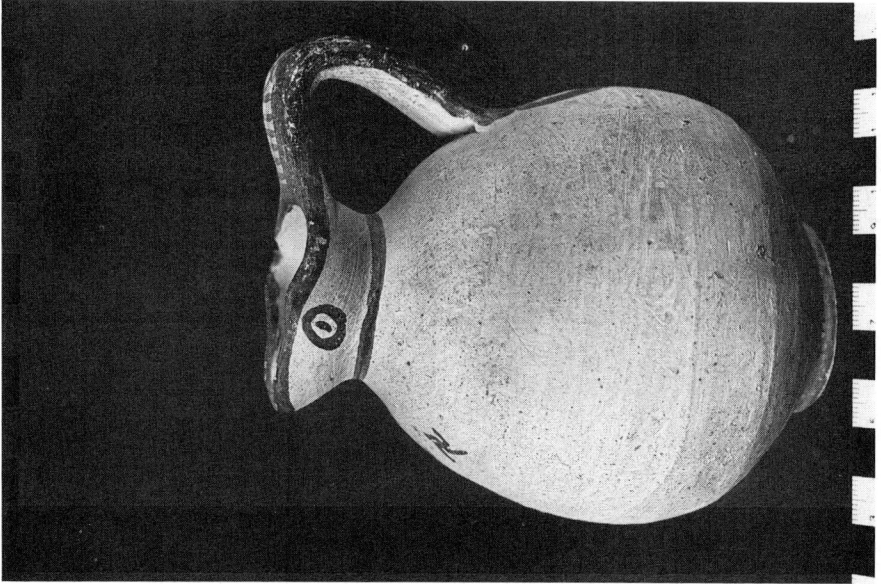

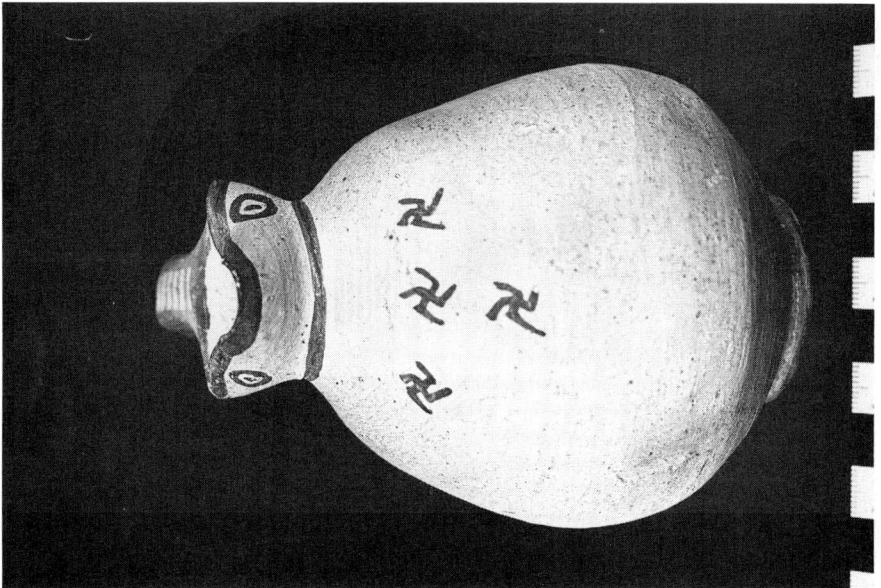

25

26

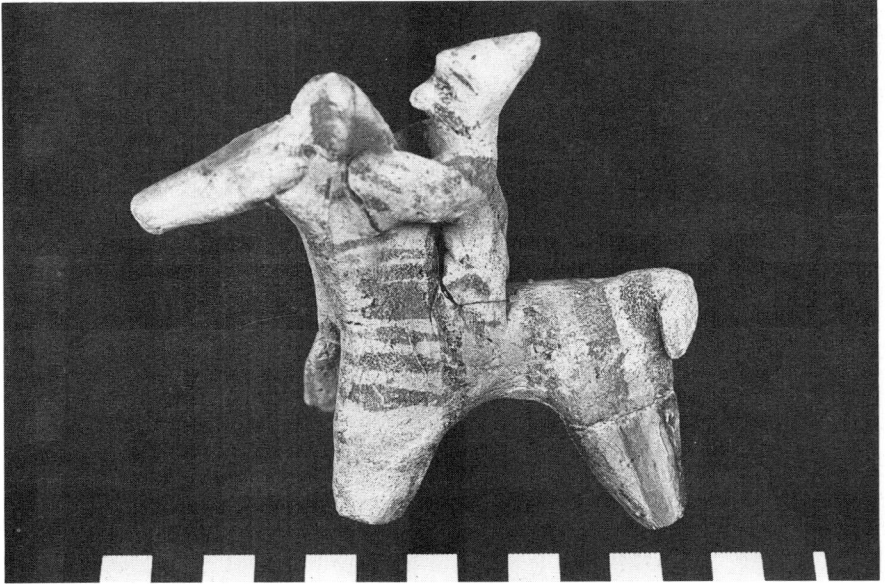

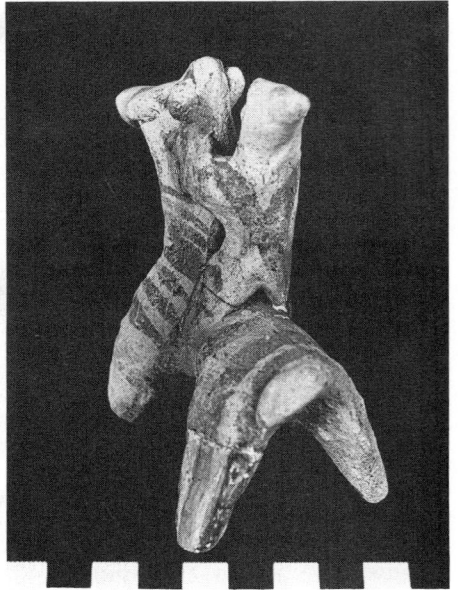

27

28

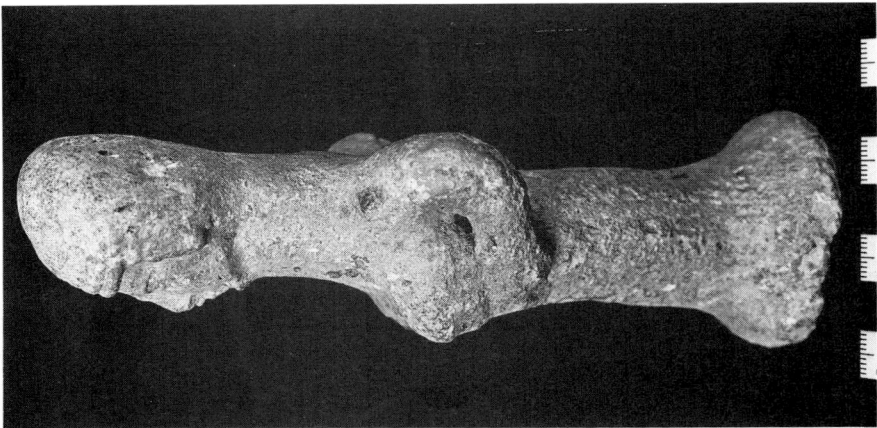

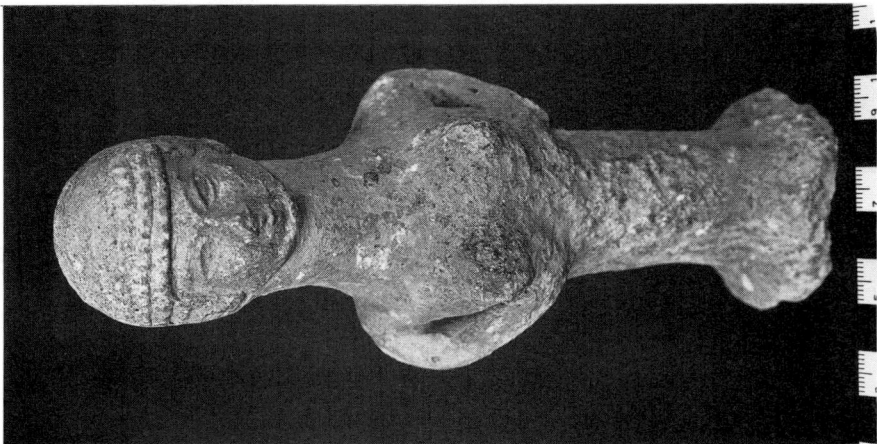

29

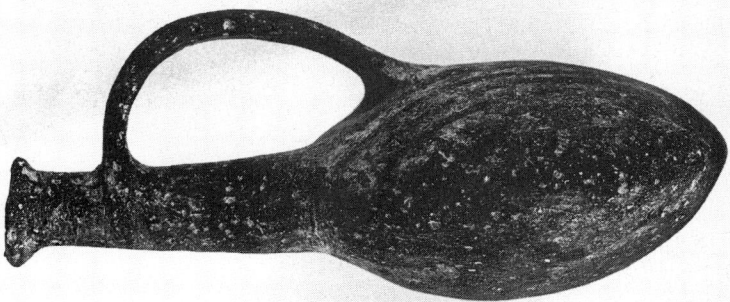

30

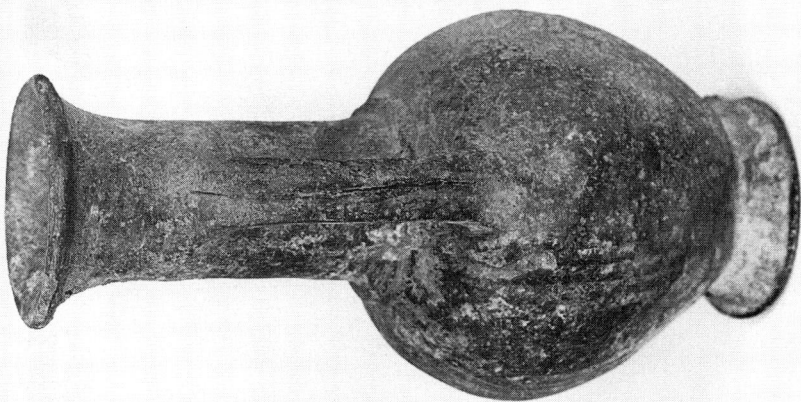

31

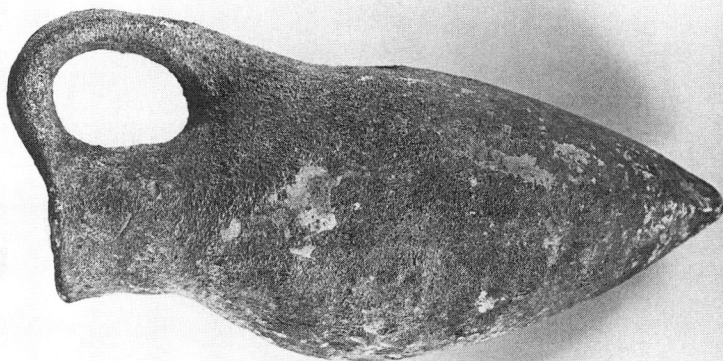

32

33

34

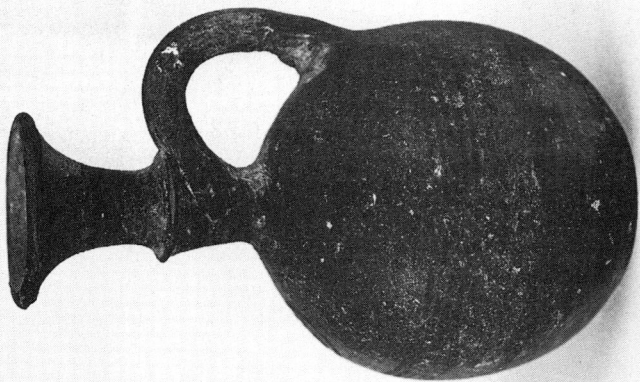

36

STUDIES IN MEDITERRANEAN ARCHAEOLOGY AND LITERATURE

Pocket-books

14 March, 1992

Edited and published by Professor Paul Åström
W. Gibsons väg 11, S-433 76 Partille
SWEDEN

1. P. Åström, Cypern – *motsättningarnas ö.*
2. R. L Murray, *The Protogeometric Style.* The First Greek Style.
3. (E. J. Holmberg, Aten. Out of print.)
4. R. Laffineur, *Les vases en métal précieux à l'époque mycénienne.*
5. (E. J. Holmberg, Delfi och Olympia. Out of print.)
6. L. Pomerance, *The Phaistos Disc.*
7. E. Wistrand, *Politik och litteratur i antikens Rom.*
8. E. J. Holmberg, *Athens.*
9. R. S. Merrillees, *Introduction to the Bronze Age Archaeology of Cyprus.*
10. E. J. Holmberg, *Delphi and Olympia.*
11. P. Åström, *Arkeologiskt detektivarbete.*
12. E. Gjerstad, *Ages and Days in Cyprus.*
13. A. Andrén, Capri – *From the Stone Age to the Tourist Age.*
14. A. Andrén, *Vår vän Horatius.*
15. M. J. Alden, *Bronze Age Fluctuations in the Argolid From the Evidence of Mycenaean Tombs.*
16. E. J. Peltenburg, *Recent Developments in the Later Prehistory of Cyprus.*
17. S. F. Kromholz, *The Bronze Age Necropolis at Ayia Paraskevi* (Nicosia).
18. Z. J. Kapera, Kinyras, Bibliography of Ancient Cyprus for the Year 1979.
19. A. Andrén, *Arkeologins marodörer.*
20. A. G. Orphanides, *Bronze Age Anthropomorphic Figurines.*
21. I. Skupinska-Lövset, *Funerary Portraiture of Roman Palestine.*
22. K. Westerberg, *Cypriote Ships From the Bronze Age to c. 500 B. C.*
23. B. A. Barletta, *Ionic Influence in Archaic Sicily.*
24. I. Pohl, *Ostia, Roms hamnstad.*
25. P. Åström, L. R. Palmer & L. Pomerance, *Studies in Aegean Chronology.*
26. J. Weingarten, *The Zakro Master and His Place in Prehistory.*
27. A. Andrén, *Orvieto.*
28. Z. J. Kapera, *Kinyras*, Bibliography of Ancient Cyprus for the Year 1978.
29. (Epiktetos. Översättning av G. Grunewald. Out of print.)
30. (Antika motiv i modern grekisk poesi. Out of print.)
31. K. -E. Sjöquist & P. Åström, Pylos: Palmprints and Palmleaves.
32. G. Säflund, *Att tyda antika bildverk.*
33. S. Sophocleous, *Atlas des représentations chypro-archaiques des divinités.*
34. C. W. Shelmerdine, *The Perfume Industry at Mycenaean Pylos.*
35. O. Vessberg, *Romersk porträttkonst.*
36. A. Andrén, *Deeds and Misdeeds in Classical Art and Antiquities.*

37. H. Hankey, *Archaeology: Artifacts and Artifiction.*
38. A. Ollfors, *Hjalmar Söderberg och antiken och andra essayer.*
39. I. Algulin, *Nyklassicism som litterär tradition.*
40. W. Culican, *Opera Selecta.*
41. (K. P. Kavafis' samlade publicerade dikter. Out of print.)
42. A. B. Knapp, *Copper Production and Divine Protection:* Archae-ology, Ideology and Social Complexity on Bronze Age Cyprus.
43. W. D. E. Coulson, *The Dark Age Pottery of Messenia.*
44. M. P. Nilsson, *Cults, Myths, Oracles and Politics in Ancient Greece.*
45. A. -M. & L. Didoff, *Fragments av tid och rum.* Antiken i konstnärligt ljus.
46. R. M. Rilke, *Briefe an Ernst Norlind.* Herausgegeben von P. Åström.
47. P. Bien, *Tre generationer av grekiska författare:* 1. *Konstantin Kavafis.* Översättning och bearbetning av G. Grunewald.
48. G. P. Shams, *Some Minor Textiles in Antiquity.*
49. G. Walberg, *Kamares.* A Study of the Character of Palatial Middle Minoan Pottery. 2nd ed.
50. Y. G. Lólos, *The Late Helladic I Pottery of the Southwestern Peloponnesos and Its Local Characteristics.*
51. J. L. Crowley, *The Aegean and the East.* An Investigation into the Transference of Artistic Motifs between the Aegean, Egypt, and the Near East in the Bronze Age.
52. *Modern grekisk poesi.* En antologi. Översättning av G. Grunewald.
53. B. Kurtén-Lindberg, *Women's Lib i Aristiophanes' Athen?*
54. S. Stuart Leach, *Subgeometric Pottery from Southern Etruria.*
55. A. Schöne, *Der Thiasos.* Eine ikonographische Untersuchung über das Gefolge des Dionysos in der attischen Vasenmalerei des 6. und 5. Jhs. v. Chr.
56-57. P. Åström (ed.), *High, Middle or Low?* Acts of an International Colloquium on Absolute chronology Held in Gothenburg 20th–22nd August 1987. Parts 1–2.
58. L. J. Bliquez, *Roman Surgical Instruments and Minor Objects in the University of Mississippi.*
59. *Horatius,* satirer och epistlar i urval. Originaltexter och översättningar av A. Andrén.
60. *N. Kazantzakis' filosofiska testamente.*
61. R. M. Rilke. *Ett urval tolkningar* av Patrik Reutersvärd.
62. O. Psychoyos, *Déplacements de la ligne de rivage et sites archéologiques dans les régions côtières de la mer Egée, au Néolithique et à l'Age du Bronze.*
63. J. P. Sartre, *Barjona eller åskans son.*
64. N. Kazantzakis, *ODYSSEEN. SÅNG I.* Översättning: G. Grunewald.
65. L. von Rosen, *Lapis lazuli in geological contexts and in ancient written sources.*
66. R. M. Rilke, *Briefe an Tora Vega Holmström.* Herausgegeben von B. Rausing und P. Åström.

67. K. Czernohaus, *Delphindarstellungen von der minoischen biz zur geometrischen Zeit.*
68. T. Rombos, *The Iconography of Attic Late Geometric II Pottery.*
69. D. N. Tripathi, *Bronzework of Mainland Greece* from c. 2600 B. C. to 1450 B. C.
70. B. Mattsson, *The Ascia Symbol on Latin Epitaphs.*
71. A. Andrén, *Latinska dikter om kärlek, lidande och död.* Originaltexter och metriska översättningar.
72. P. Warren, *Minoan Religion as Ritual Action.*
73. M. C. Astour, *Hittite History and Absolute Chronology of the Bronze Age.*
74. G. Säflund, *Etrusker – vad menade ni egentligen?* Etruskiskt bildspråk – symbol och mening.
75. J. M. Webb, *Ritual Architecture, Iconography and Practice in the Late Cypriote Bronze Age.* In preparation.
76. M. Tsipopoulou, *Archaeological Survey at Aghia Photia, Siteia.*
77. E. Stavrianopoulou, *Untersuchungen zur Struktur des Reiches von Pylos.* Die Stellung der Ortschaften im Lichte der Linear B-Texte.
78. J. C. Overbeck, *The Bronze Age Pottery from the Kastro at Paros.*
79. C. Vasdaris, *Das dorische Kapitell in der hellenistisch-römischen Zeit im östlichen Mittelmeerraum.* In preparation.
80. P. Åström (ed.), *High, Middle or Low?* Acts of an International Colloquium on Absolute Chronology Held in Gothenburg 20th–22nd August 1987. Part 3.
81. B. Lindegård & P. Åström, *Hippokrates och vår tids sjukvård.*
82. K. -E. Sjöquist & P. Åström, *Knossos: Keepers and Kneaders.*
83. Ovidius, *Tristia.* Översättning av J. W. Köhler.
84. J. Weinstein Balthazar, *Copper and Bronze Workning in Early Through Middle Bronze Age Cyprus.*
85. J. Gifford, *The Geoarchaeology of Hala Sultan Tekke.* In preparation.
86. H. Hjelmqvist, *A Cereal Find From Old Etruria.*
87. E. J. Holmberg, *The Red-Line Painter and the Workshop of the Acheloos Painter.*
88. N. Kelly Cooper, *The Development of Roof Revetment in the Peloponnese.*
89. *Johannes Edfelt och antiken.* Med kommentarer av P. Åström.
90. *Gunnar Ekelöf och Gottfrid Walldén, Brevväxling.* Utgiven av P. Åström.
91. P. Åström, *Gunnar Ekelöf och antiken.* In preparation.
92. *Jeno Platthy and Antiquity.* An Anthology edited by P. Åstorm. In preparation.
93. L. von Rosen, *Lapis lazuli in Archaeological Contexts.*
94. A. Andrén, *Minnen från min forntid.*
95. C. Lambrou-Phillipson, *Hellenorientalia.* The Near Eastern Presence in the Bronze Age Aegean, ca. 3000–1100 B. C. Interconnections based on the Material Record and the Written Evidence plus Orientalia. A Catalogue of Egyptian, Mesopotamian, Mitannian, Syro-Palestinian, Cypriot and Asia Minor Objects From the Bronze Age Aegean.